THE
LONDON BAPTIST
CONFESSION
OF 1689

INTRODUCTION BY PATRICK ABENDROTH

WELL PUBLICATIONS

THE LONDON BAPTIST CONFESSION OF 1689

Introduction Copyright © 2017
by Patrick Abendroth

Published by Well Publications
7940 State Street Omaha, Nebraska 68122

Design and Layout
Erin Pille

Printed in the United States of America

All rights reserved. No part of this publication may be reproduced, stored in a retrieval system, or transmitted in any form by an means, electronic, mechanical, photocopy, recording, or otherwise, without the prior permission of the publisher, except as provided by USA copyright law.

Scripture quotations are from the ESV® Bible (The Holy Bible, English Standard Version®), copyright © 2001 by Crossway, a publishing ministry of Good News Publishers. Used by permission. All rights reserved.

Paperback ISBN: 978-0-9760804-1-1

TABLE OF CONTENTS

7 Introduction

21 The Holy Scriptures

27 God & The Holy Trinity

29 God's Decree

33 Creation

35 Divine Providence

39 The Fall Of Man, Sin, & Its Punishment

41 God's Covenant

43 Christ The Mediator

47 Free Will

49 Effectual Calling

51 Justification

53 Adoption

55 Sanctification

57 Saving Faith

59 Repentance & Salvation

61 Good Works

65 The Perseverance Of The Saints

67 Assurance Of Salvation

69 The Law Of God

73 The Gospel & Its Influence

75 Christian Liberty & Liberty Of Conscience

77 Worship & The Sabbath Day

81 Lawful Oaths & Vows

83 The Civil Magistrate

85 Marriage

87 The Church

93 The Communion Of Saints

95 Baptism & The Lord's Supper

97 Baptism

99 The Lord's Supper

103 Man's State After Death, & The Resurrection

105 The Last Judgment

107 Resources

INTRODUCTION
BY PATRICK ABENDROTH

If you believe in the Trinity then you believe in the legitimacy of Christian confessions such as the one you hold in your hands (or are reading on a screen). Yes, I am attempting to be provocative by suggesting to know what you believe, but please bear with me long enough to explain.

I say that if you believe in the Trinity then you believe in confessions not because the triune nature of God is not revealed in the Bible. It definitely is. I say this because the word "Trinity" as well as its formal meaning—one God eternally and simultaneously existing in three persons—is never stated as such in any specific verse of the Bible. Instead, "Trinity" reflects an *interpretation* of the biblical revelation, the interpretation that Christians have agreed upon and at times admirably defended against formidable opposition. This is the essence of a Christian confession. A Christian confession is an agreed upon (to confess means to agree) understanding/interpretation of something that is considered vital to the Christian faith.

A classic example of an early Christian confession is the one quoted by the Apostle Paul in his first letter to Timothy. It reads,

> Great indeed, we confess, is the mystery of godliness: He was manifested in the flesh, vindicated by the Spirit, seen by angels, proclaimed among the nations, believed on in the world, taken up in glory (1 Timothy 3:16).

Besides offering a wonderful summary of gospel truth, the quotation by Paul gives evidence of the legitimate utilization of such tools by the Christian church.

For centuries Christians have found such agreements to be a vital help in discipleship. The greatest opponents of Christian confessions have historically been opponents of biblical Christianity such as Arians. Adversaries have objected to the need for written explanations of what the Bible means by what it says and have hid heresy behind a disingenuous "we only believe the Bible" disguise.

Many well meaning Christians today are not aware of the important role that confessions have played in the history of God's people. It is therefore fairly common to assume that the most biblical people shunned confessions and the heretics utilized them. In reality, it has often been the exact opposite. This misinformed mindset has greatly weakened the church. The following introduction and confession are offered in an effort to highlight the importance of historic confessions for the glory of Christ and the good of His people.

The intended readership of this introduction is not the scholar or individual looking for detailed explanations of the history and content of confessions in general or of this one in particular. There are other valuable resources available to meet such needs. The aim here is to introduce believers to the significance of what has been called confessional Christianity. Readers of the confession will notice occasional notes of explanation. These are provided because general clarification seems necessary to bridge a historical, cultural, or language gap. On other occasions notes are included in order to express differing opinions.

Now we will consider some of the more vital benefits of a confession like this one. The benefits of a historic Protestant confession we will highlight include:

1. It Expresses Humility.

2. It Avoids the Cult of Personality.

3. It Complements *Sola Scriptura.*

4. It Distinguishes Between Law and Gospel.

5. It Unifies Christians.

6. It Expresses Appropriate Distinctions.

7. It Allows Reasonable Freedom.

8. It Demonstrates Transparency.

9. It Equips for Discipleship.

Following the discussion of the nine benefits of confessions I will make some brief comments about the London Baptist Confession of 1689. That will conclude our introduction to the confession. Some recommended resources for further consideration are included at the back of this book. Now for the vital benefits.

1. It Expresses Humility

It is difficult to imagine anyone today actually claiming to be the first Christian or that authentic Christianity started in our lifetime. But a more subtle form of this mindset does exist. This way of thinking exists when believers fail to consider those who have come before us. More specifically, when we fail to consider previous conclusions about Christian doctrines, we demonstrate what amounts to a lack of humility. Not only have there been millions of Christians before the twenty-first century, but they have enjoyed the ministry of the Holy Spirit.

Jesus promised the disciples that His Spirit would lead them into all the truth (John 16:13). While this promise may be intended specifically for the disciples as they would be His Apostles entrusted with a unique apostolic ministry, we can at least acknowledge that Jesus promised His Spirit to all believers and that some would lead, guide, and shepherd the church. This Spirit has been uniquely working in the church and teaching the people of God for millennia. The church has given her best efforts, guided by the Spirit, to make conclusions regarding major theological questions. For us to ignore historic confessions and act like we are the very first people to have the teaching of the Holy Spirit is just plain silly.

A confession like this one connects us to the past and more importantly, to the work of the Spirit in the church. I realize that this challenges the spirit of the age (I'm thinking of Ford's saying: "History is more or less bunk"). But far better than wisdom from the spirit of the age is the wisdom from the Spirit of the ages! When we consider the specifics of this confession from 1689 we learn that its drafters went out of their way to sound as much like other older confessions as they possibly could. They wanted to be essentially unified with the past as they believed that God had worked in great ways and that His work was not to be ignored.

This does not require that the Bible be under the authority of history for history is far from heresy free. But wisdom calls for noting how the Lord has guided His church through history using His word, the Bible. Additionally, the church today can avoid falling into countless theological deviations that have historically been tested and found unbiblical. Such avoidance is the fruit of humbly paying attention to what has happened before our time. Conversely, where pride keeps us looking only inward and to ourselves, it is no wonder that we fall (Proverbs 16:18).

2. It Avoids the Cult of Personality

Ask a conservative evangelical which personality cult he or she is a member of and you can expect a puzzled look in response. No one thinks they belong to a personality cult, especially those who think of themselves as simply Christians who believe the Bible and nothing else. But given that every Christian has opinions about what the Bible means by what it says regarding any given topic, everyone ends up with a theological position regardless of whether they are aware of it or not. We have already discussed this at some length so I will not belabor the point here. But I will say that with a move away from the use of historic confessions and toward a supposed "Bible only" biblicism, theological positions and systems have not disappeared in the least. But what has happened is an increased ignorance of just what theological position one is actually aligned with. In addition, the greatest breeding ground for personality cults is the "we just believe the Bible" environment.

Apart from confessional Christianity, whole congregations could potentially affirm a local pastor's deviant understandings of major doctrines. Then on a larger scale when celebrity preachers promote theological novelty or worse under the seemingly pristine label of "biblicism," the cult grows exponentially and its members blindly follow. I have experienced this firsthand as a young Christian. I affirmed novel doctrines because my favorite Bible teacher taught them. Then when he changed his views to align with what confessions had said for centuries, I changed (along with what I would assume to be most of his followers). In hindsight, I am thankful for the changes. Maturity is good. However, my following and the following of countless others revealed our true allegiance. In the name of biblicism, we were shown to be in actuality most devoted to a persuasive leader. The lone teacher was the theological standard even if I would not have wanted to admit it.

It is far better to have a theological standard that is the historic product of a great multitude of biblical scholars and has been agreed upon (i.e. confessed) by countless Christian men and women over the centuries. The Bible alone remains the only inspired revelation from God by which all creeds, confessions, and traditions must be evaluated, but the allusion of being purely biblical without either accidentally or intentionally aligning with a theological position is naïvely dangerous. As has been said by others, it is the person who thinks that he or she has no tradition who is most enslaved to it.

3. It Complements *Sola Scriptura*

One of the hallmarks coming from the Protestant Reformation is known as *Sola Scriptura* (Latin for Scripture Alone). Unfortunately, a hallmark of current evangelicalism is utilizing the Reformation slogan for something vastly different from what the actual Reformers intended. *Sola Scriptura* affirms that the Bible is the sole source of special revelation and sole infallible authority. This is markedly different from saying that the Bible is the *only* authority. The Reformers affirmed the former and denied the latter as they affirmed legitimate institutional authority such as church authority and government authority. The Reformers likewise did not reject tradition. What they did was turn to the Bible as the source by which tradition must be evaluated.

Historian Carl Trueman aptly observes that

> "Thoughtful Protestants then, and ever since, have understood the Reformers as arguing for what we might call a tradition that is normed by Scripture. In other words, Protestants know that they use language and conceptual terminology not found explicitly in the Bible; but they understand such are useful in understanding what Scripture says and, at the point where they are found to be inadequate for this task, or even to contradict Scripture, there they must be modified or abandoned. The same is true of the creeds and confessions of the church, which are, one might say, the most concentrated deposits of tradition, as affirmed by the church."[1]

4. It Distinguishes Between Law and Gospel

One of the truly watershed outcomes of the Protestant Reformation was the recovery of the clear distinction that the Bible makes between the law of God and the gospel of God. The former is what God requires (loving God and neighbor appropriately) and the latter is what God provides in Christ (fulfillment of the law). Such a clear and important distinction was seen and highlighted by the likes of Martin Luther and John Calvin. It was also highlighted in the Protestant confessions that followed.

This distinction is vital and must be maintained or the gospel will be distorted into something far different. Confessions such as this one uphold the good requirement of God's law as well as the fulfillment of the divine law by Jesus. In addition, the confession maintains the biblical call for justified sinners to follow the law in a spirit of gratitude rather than out of fear of judgment. After all, there is no condemnation for those who are in Christ.

These categories of law and gospel are commonly confused or collapsed into one in our day as they were in medieval times. This is extremely dangerous as it ends up compromising both the gospel and the law. Yet such compromise is not necessary and the confession offers mature guidance toward that end.

5. It Unifies Christians

A confession by definition is unifying. After all, confess means to agree which is another way of saying unite. So subscribers to a given confession are united. Looking to the present, they are unified with other believers who also affirm that the specified interpretation expressed in the confession is in concert with what the Bible intends. This can be enjoyed on the level of a local congregation as well as on a broader scale where other congregations in other places affirm the confession.

One practical example of confessional unity would be that all those who affirm this confession are united in affirming the finality of special revelation from God. Therefore agreement can be enjoyed in affirming the ultimate authority of the Bible as opposed to the subjective whims or imaginations of men and women. This is only to name one example.

Such a unity can also look forward. We can look forward and see the confession as a practical means for passing on the faith to the next generation. Circumstances will change and challenges will come in different forms, but the faith that has been delivered once and for all will not change (Jude 3).

When a local congregation welcomes a new pastor, after the last one served them for decades, a confession provides a bond of unity between the pastor and congregation. The expectations of both pastor and flock will be guided by the objectivity of the confessional standard rather than differing theological convictions that one may intend for the other to adopt. Surely there will be change and change can be very good. But the change does not need to come on the level of fundamental doctrines. If the congregation subscribes to the confession and the new pastor does also, they enjoy the unity from a common confession.

A unity with believers who have gone before us is another great blessing, which has already been discussed.

6. It Expresses Appropriate Distinctions

Complementing the unity of confessions is their ability to express distinction. A historic confession such as this one includes much that is the same as other confessions before it shows distinction. For example, the statements concerning the person of Christ align with the Nicene Creed (A.D. 325) and the Athanasian Creed (A.D.

500). But with the recovery of the gospel at the time of the Protestant Reformation there arose the need to express specifically where the theological differences existed. This was especially true in areas that related to the nature of humanity, the work of Christ, and the way in which God saves sinners. Such expression came in the form of confessions such as the Augsburg (A.D. 1530) of Lutheranism, the Belgic (A.D. 1561) of the Reformed, and the Westminster (A.D. 1647) of the Presbyterians. These confessions intentionally agree with those that had come before them in so far as they could. They therefore were not seeking to start something new or even state something in a new way. After all, they recognized the work of the Spirit in ages past.

However, they could not agree with specific doctrines that arose as the church had drifted away from the biblical realities of salvation being by grace alone through faith alone because of Christ alone. Therefore the church desired to affirm the past, but not to the degree of ignoring the explicit teaching of the Bible. When it came to this, they had to protest. With the necessary protest came the Protestant Reformation and its confessions that formally expressed distinction from Romanism. In this sense the Protestants were compelled to show that the Roman religion's teachings no longer reflected the catholic (universal) church.

If you read the Westminster Confession for example you will notice that a deliberate contrast is being made. There is contrast between its adherents and those promoting salvation by some form of human achievement. Whether they be of the papal or Arminian persuasion, the distinction was necessary. The distinction demonstrated faithfulness to the gospel of grace. The London Baptist Confession is very similar to the Westminster. The most striking difference is in the area of baptism.

Those who were convinced that baptism was reserved for those who had made a conscious profession of faith or believer's baptism found it necessary to have a confession. These Christians aimed to make it clear that they were by and large in agreement with the Presbyterians and like the Presbyterians were not seeking to disregard the working of God in the past. They were not disregarding things that had been universally accepted by believers and articulated in their confessions. In addition, these who were committed to reserving baptism for believers sought to distance themselves from certain Anabaptists. Anabaptists had a reputation for overreacting to anything previously affirmed by Christians including things like the Bible, Pastors, and the Trinity. To oversimplify, they were prone to reject anything and everything taught by Roman Catholicism. They were counted as fanatics. The London Baptist Confession sought to distinguish its subscribers from the fanatical while also expressing biblical convictions regarding the recipients of baptism.

7. It Allows Reasonable Freedom

One of my favorite things about the use of a confession like this one by a local church is the freedom it affords. This may sound peculiar upon first hearing it. After all, doesn't a confession establish boundaries? Yes, it does establish boundaries but such boundaries are simultaneously freeing. They are freeing because everyone from the preacher to youth workers can enjoy what amounts to great freedom provided that they work within the framework of the confession.

Anyone who has ever sought to teach in the local church and wanted to act in such a way that supported and complemented the overall ministry focus of the church can see the appeal to the freedom within confessional boundaries. Those teaching can experience relative freedom in teaching various biblical texts and know that their teaching is supporting the overall ministry of the church as they remain within the agreed upon theological framework of the confession. This enjoyment of freedom also extends to the preacher. If he has joined the congregation in affirming the confession, he too can enjoy such reasonable freedom.

The congregation can also experience the confidence in knowing that their pastor has freedom provided he "colors within the lines" so to speak. They need not be forever wondering whether or not the preaching crosses the line into the novel. I am not suggestion that believers should ever fully let their guard down as they are called to be discerning. But, employing a confession can help to foster an atmosphere where appropriate freedom can be appreciated.

8. It Demonstrates Transparency

A confession shows forthrightness because it is a written document. It is a written document expressing a church's understanding of God and His ways in light of the Bible's teaching. As a written document a confession can be objectively analyzed, criticized, rejected, or affirmed.

When it is said that an organization or individual has no theology or doctrine other than the Bible it can sound impressive. What purists! Or so it is thought. But when asked who Jesus is or what the gospel is, the one responding instantly reveals that he or she does have a theological position. If someone is asked to affirm or deny that salvation is by grace alone through faith alone in the finished work of Christ alone, the affirmation or denial will reveal a theological position. There is also good practical and historical reasoning behind asking such a question. For among those who passionately affirm the truthfulness of the Bible there are those who believe that salvation is by grace alone through faith alone because of Christ alone and there are those who do not. What is revealed in whether a person agrees with or rejects the statement is one's *understanding* of the Bible. Therefore the way one answers the question can show if someone is *confessing* the same understanding as other believers or not.

When an organization refuses to provide a written confession, there is a lack of transparency.

9. It Equips for Discipleship

Protestants recognize their reformation as a work of divine providence. Far from seeing the sixteenth century event as the beginning of their religion, the Reformation is viewed as the work of God in recovering the gospel of Jesus Christ. One of the formidable challenges resulting from the Reformation was the challenge of discipleship. With all ties to Romanism being cut, now what? They were wrong about so many issues relating to the work of Christ, the gospel, and the Christian life. But where had Rome remained biblical if anywhere and what did the Bible actually teach regarding gospel related doctrines? For the spiritual health of Christians, the church, congregations, and pastors, confessions were drafted, affirmed, and utilized.

Several features of the confessions made them exceptional tools for the discipleship that was so important for the time. Not only were they theologically robust, biblically sound, historically informed, and pastorally mature, the confessions were to the point and relatively simple. Such a balance provided a great tool for instruction. It is this same balance that makes this confession ideal for discipling believers today. As a pastor who has given much of my life to helping people grow in their knowledge of God, His ways, and

His world, I have found that utilizing a confession is immeasurably better, not to mention easier, as a starting point and theological baseline than a thousand page systematic theology textbook.

Conclusion

I heartily agree with Charles H. Spurgeon the esteemed evangelist and pastor regarding this London Confession—it is an "excellent list of doctrines" and "is the most excellent epitome of the things most surely believed among us." [2] I also share Mr. Spurgeon's desire that this "small volume may aid the cause of the glorious gospel by testifying plainly what are its leading doctrines." [3] He said this a century and a half after the confession was written because he viewed it as the most valuable tool to complement his preaching of the Bible in helping the believers entrusted to his care. A century and a half later I find my pastor's heart sharing these convictions. The faith that has been once and for all delivered to the saints is expressed and summarized in unrivaled excellence in this confession.

The Bible itself is supreme as the confession itself boldly states. So in no way should the proverbial tail wag the dog. Yet I believe that the confession expresses and articulates an understanding of the Bible that is faithful to the text of Scripture, historically mature, and best fit for equipping the people of God today.

Patrick Abendroth
October 2017

---

[1] Carl R. Trueman, *The Creedal Imperative*
(Wheaton: Good News Publishers, 2012), Kindle Electronic Edition: Locations 192-198.

[2] Lewis A. Drummond, *Spurgeon: Prince of Preachers*
(Grand Rapids: Kregel Publications, 1992), 222.

[3] http://www.reformed.org/documents/index.html?mainframe=http://www.reformed.org/documents/baptist_1689.html

CHAPTER 1:
THE HOLY SCRIPTURES

1. The Holy Scripture is the only sufficient, certain, and infallible rule of all saving knowledge, faith, and obedience,[1] although the light of nature, and the works of creation and providence do so far manifest the goodness, wisdom, and power of God, as to leave men inexcusable; yet they are not sufficient to give that knowledge of God and His will which is necessary unto salvation.[2] Therefore it pleased the Lord at sundry times and in diversified manners to reveal Himself, and to declare (that) His will unto His church;[3] and afterward for the better preserving and propagating of the truth, and for the more sure establishment and comfort of the church against the corruption of the flesh, and the malice of Satan, and of the world, to commit the same wholly unto writing; which makes the Holy Scriptures to be most necessary, those former ways of God's revealing His will unto His people being now completed.[4]

2. Under the name of Holy Scripture, or the Word of God written, are now contained all the books of the Old and New Testaments, which are these:

THE OLD TESTAMENT

Genesis	Joshua	1 Kings
Exodus	Judges	2 Kings
Leviticus	Ruth	1 Chronicles
Numbers	1 Samuel	2 Chronicles
Deuteronomy	2 Samuel	Ezra

THE OLD TESTAMENT (CONT.)

Nehemiah	Lamentations	Nahum
Esther	Ezekiel	Habakkuk
Job	Daniel	Zephaniah
Psalms	Hosea	Haggai
Proverbs	Joel	Zechariah
Ecclesiastes	Amos	Malachi
Song of Solomon	Obadiah	
Isaiah	Jonah	
Jeremiah	Micah	

THE NEW TESTAMENT

Matthew	Ephesians	James
Mark	Philippians	1 Peter
Luke	Colossians	2 Peter
John	1 Thessalonians	1 John
Acts (of the Apostles)	2 Thessalonians	2 John
	1 Timothy	3 John
Romans	2 Timothy	Jude
1 Corinthians	Titus	Revelation
2 Corinthians	Philemon	
Galatians	Hebrews	

All of which are given by the inspiration of God, to be the rule of faith and life.[5]

3. The books commonly called Apocrypha, not being of divine inspiration, are no part of the canon or rule of the Scripture, and, therefore, are of no authority to the church of God, nor to be any otherwise approved or made use of than other human writings.[6]

4. The authority of the Holy Scripture, for which it ought to be believed, depends not upon the testimony of any man or church, but wholly upon God (who is truth itself), the author thereof; therefore it is to be received because it is the Word of God.[7]

5. We may be moved and induced by the testimony of the church of God to a high and reverent esteem of the Holy Scriptures; and the heavenliness of the matter, the efficacy of the doctrine, and the majesty of the style, the consent of all the parts, the scope of the whole (which is to give all glory to God), the full discovery it makes of the only way of man's salvation, and many other incomparable excellencies, and entire perfections thereof, are arguments whereby it does abundantly evidence itself to be the Word of God; yet notwithstanding, our full persuasion and assurance of the infallible truth, and divine authority thereof, is from the inward work of the Holy Spirit bearing witness by and with the Word in our hearts.[8]

6. The whole counsel of God concerning all things necessary for His own glory, man's salvation, faith and life, is either expressly set down or necessarily contained in the Holy Scripture: unto which nothing at any time is to be added, whether by new revelation of the Spirit, or traditions of men.[9] Nevertheless, we acknowledge the inward illumination of the Spirit of God to be necessary for the saving understanding of such things as are revealed in the Word,[10] and that there are some circumstances concerning the worship of God, and government of the church, common to human actions and societies, which are to be ordered by the light of nature and Christian prudence, according to the general rules of the Word, which are always to be observed.[11]

7. All things in Scripture are not alike plain in themselves, nor alike clear unto all;[12] yet those things which are necessary to be known, believed and observed for salvation, are so clearly propounded and opened in some place of Scripture or other, that not only the learned, but the unlearned, in a due use of ordinary means, may attain to a sufficient understanding of them.[13]

8. The Old Testament in Hebrew (which was the native language of the people of God of old),[14] and the New Testament in Greek (which at the time of the writing of it was most generally known to the nations), being immediately inspired by God, and by His singular care and providence kept pure in all ages, are therefore authentic; so as in all controversies of religion, the church is finally to appeal to them.[15] But because these original tongues are not known to all the people of God, who have a right unto, and interest in the Scriptures, and are commanded in the fear of God to read,[16] and search them,[17] therefore they are to be translated into the vulgar language of every nation unto which they come,[18] that the Word of God dwelling plentifully in all, they may worship Him in an acceptable manner, and through patience and comfort of the Scriptures may have hope.[19]

9. The infallible rule of interpretation of Scripture is the Scripture itself; and therefore when there is a question about the true and full sense of any Scripture (which are not many, but one), it must be searched by other places that speak more clearly.[20]

10. The supreme judge, by which all controversies of religion are to be determined, and all decrees of councils, opinions of ancient writers, doctrines of men, and private spirits, are to be examined, and in whose sentence we are to rest, can be no

other but the Holy Scripture delivered by the Spirit, into which Scripture so delivered, our faith is finally resolved.[21]

---

1 2 Timothy 3:15-17; Isaiah 8:20; Luke 16:29,31; Ephesians. 2:20 **2** Romans 1:19-21, 2:14-15; Psalm 19:1-3 **3** Hebrews 1:1 **4** Proverbs 22:19-21; Romans 15:4; 2 Peter 1:19-20 **5** 2 Timothy 3:16 **6** Luke 24:27,44; Romans 3:2 **7** 2 Peter 1:19-21; 2 Timothy 3:16; 1 Thessalonians 2:13; 1 John 5:9 **8** John 16:13-14; 1 Corinthians 2:10-12; 1 John 2:20,27 **9** 2 Timothy 3:15-17; Galatians 1:8-9 **10** John 6:45; 1 Corinthians 2:9-12 **11** 1 Corinthians 11:13-14; 1 Corinthians 14:26,40 **12** 2 Peter 3:16 **13** Psalm 19:7; Psalm 119:130 **14** Romans 3:2 **15** Isaiah 8:20 **16** Acts 15:15 **17** John 5:39 **18** 1 Corinthians 14:6,9,11-12,24,28 **19** Colossians 3:16 **20** 2 Peter 1:20-21; Acts 15:15-16 **21** Matthew 22:29,31-32; Ephesians 2:20; Acts 28:23

CHAPTER 2:
GOD & THE HOLY TRINITY

1. The Lord our God is but one only living and true God;[1] whose subsistence is in and of Himself,[2] infinite in being and perfection; whose essence cannot be comprehended by any but Himself;[3] a most pure spirit,[4] invisible, without body, parts, or passions, who only hath immortality, dwelling in the light which no man can approach unto;[5] who is immutable,[6] immense,[7] eternal,[8] incomprehensible, almighty,[9] every way infinite, most holy,[10] most wise, most free, most absolute; working all things according to the counsel of His own immutable and most righteous will,[11] for His own glory;[12] most loving, gracious, merciful, long-suffering, abundant in goodness and truth, forgiving iniquity, transgression, and sin; the rewarder of them that diligently seek Him,[13] and withal most just and terrible in His judgments,[14] hating all sin,[15] and who will by no means clear the guilty.[16]

2. God, having all life,[17] glory,[18] goodness,[19] blessedness, in and of Himself, is alone in and unto Himself all-sufficient, not standing in need of any creature which He hath made, nor deriving any glory from them,[20] but only manifesting His own glory in, by, unto, and upon them; He is the alone fountain of all being, of whom, through whom, and to whom are all things,[21] and He hath most sovereign dominion over all creatures, to do by them, for them, or upon them, whatsoever Himself pleases;[22] in His sight all things are open and manifest,[23] His knowledge is infinite, infallible, and independent

upon the creature, so as nothing is to Him contingent or uncertain;[24] He is most holy in all His counsels, in all His works,[25] and in all His commands; to Him is due from angels and men, whatsoever worship,[26] service, or obedience, as creatures they owe unto the Creator, and whatever He is further pleased to require of them.

3. In this divine and infinite Being there are three subsistences, the Father, the Word or Son, and Holy Spirit,[27] of one substance, power, and eternity, each having the whole divine essence, yet the essence undivided:[28] the Father is of none, neither begotten nor proceeding; the Son is eternally begotten of the Father;[29] the Holy Spirit proceeding from the Father and the Son;[30] all infinite, without beginning, therefore but one God, who is not to be divided in nature and being, but distinguished by several peculiar relative properties and personal relations; which doctrine of the Trinity is the foundation of all our communion with God, and comfortable dependence on Him.

---

[1] 1 Corinthians 8:4,6; Deuteronomy 6:4 [2] Jeremiah 10:10; Isaiah 48:12
[3] Exodus 3:14 [4] John 4:24 [5] 1 Timothy 1:17; Deuteronomy 4:15-16
[6] Malachi 3:6 [7] 1 Kings 8:27; Jeremiah 23:23 [8] Psalm 90:2 [9] Genesis 17:1
[10] Isaiah 6:3 [11] Psalm 115:3; Isaiah 46:10 [12] Proverbs 16:4; Romans 11:36
[13] Exodus 34:6-7; Hebrews 11:6 [14] Nehemiah 9:32-33 [15] Psalm 5:5-6
[16] Exodus 34:7; Nahum 1:2-3 [17] John 5:26 [18] Psalm 148:13 [19] Psalm 119:68
[20] Job 22:2-3 [21] Romans 11:34-36 [22] Daniel 4:25,34-35 [23] Hebrews 4:13
[24] Ezekiel 11:5; Acts 15:18 [25] Psalm 145:17 [26] Revelation 5:12-14
[27] 1 John 5:7; Matthew 28:19; 2 Corinthians 13:14 [28] Exodus 3:14; John 14:11; I Corinthians 8:6 [29] John 1:14,18 [30] John 15:26; Galatians 4:6

CHAPTER 3:
GOD'S DECREE

1. God hath decreed in himself, from all eternity, by the most wise and holy counsel of His own will, freely and unchangeably, all things, whatsoever comes to pass;[1] yet so as thereby is God neither the author of sin nor hath fellowship with any therein;[2] nor is violence offered to the will of the creature, nor yet is the liberty or contingency of second causes taken away, but rather established;[3] in which appears His wisdom in disposing all things, and power and faithfulness in accomplishing His decree.[4]

2. Although God knoweth whatsoever may or can come to pass, upon all supposed conditions,[5] yet hath He not decreed anything, because He foresaw it as future, or as that which would come to pass upon such conditions.[6]

3. By the decree of God, for the manifestation of His glory, some men and angels are predestined, or foreordained to eternal life through Jesus Christ,[7] to the praise of His glorious grace;[8] others being left to act in their sin to their just condemnation, to the praise of His glorious justice.[9]

4. These angels and men thus predestined and foreordained, are particularly and unchangeably designed, and their number so certain and definite, that it cannot be either increased or diminished.[10]

5. Those of mankind that are predestined to life, God, before the foundation of the world was laid, according to His eternal and immutable purpose, and the secret counsel and good pleasure of His will, hath chosen in Christ unto everlasting glory, out of His mere free grace and love,[11] without any other thing in the creature as a condition or cause moving Him thereunto.[12]

6. As God hath appointed the elect unto glory, so He hath, by the eternal and most free purpose of His will, foreordained all the means thereunto;[13] wherefore they who are elected, being fallen in Adam, are redeemed by Christ,[14] are effectually called unto faith in Christ, by His Spirit working in due season, are justified, adopted, sanctified,[15] and kept by His power through faith unto salvation;[16] neither are any other redeemed by Christ, or effectually called, justified, adopted, sanctified, and saved, but the elect only.[17]

7. The doctrine of the high mystery of predestination is to be handled with special prudence and care, that men attending the will of God revealed in His Word, and yielding obedience thereunto, may, from the certainty of their effectual vocation, be assured of their eternal election;[18] so shall this doctrine afford matter of praise,[19] reverence, and admiration of God, and of humility,[20] diligence, and abundant consolation to all that sincerely obey the gospel.[21]

---

[1] Isaiah 46:10; Ephesians 1:11; Hebrews 6:17; Romans 9:15,18 [2] James 1:13; 1 John 1:5 [3] Acts 4:27-28; John 19:11 [4] Numbers 23:19; Ephesians 1:3-5
[5] Acts 15:18 [6] Romans 9:11,13,16,18 [7] I Timothy 5:21; Matthew 25:34
[8] Ephesians 1:5-6 [9] Romans 9:22-23; Jude 4 [10] 2 Timothy 2:19; John 13:18
[11] Ephesians 1:4,9,11; Romans 8:30; 2 Timothy 1:9; I Thessalonians 5:9
[12] Romans 9:13,16; Ephesians 2:5,12 [13] 1 Peter 1:2; 2 Thessalonians 2:13

14 1 Thessalonians 5:9-10 **15** Romans 8:30; 2 Thessalonians 2:13 **16** 1 Peter 1:5 **17** John 10:26, 17:9, 6:64 **18** 1 Thessalonians 1:4-5; 2 Peter 1:10 **19** Ephesians 1:6; Romans 11:33 **20** Romans 11:5-6,20 **21** Luke 10:20

CHAPTER 4:
CREATION

1. In the beginning it pleased God the Father, Son, and Holy Spirit,[1] for the manifestation of the glory of His eternal power,[2] wisdom, and goodness, to create or make the world, and all things therein, whether visible or invisible, in the space of six days, and all very good.[3]

2. After God had made all other creatures, He created man, male and female,[4] with reasonable and immortal souls,[5] rendering them fit unto that life to God for which they were created; being made after the image of God, in knowledge, righteousness, and true holiness;[6] having the law of God written in their hearts,[7] and power to fulfill it, and yet under a possibility of transgressing, being left to the liberty of their own will, which was subject to change.[8]

3. Besides the law written in their hearts, they received a command not to eat of the tree of knowledge of good and evil,[9] which while they kept, they were happy in their communion with God, and had dominion over the creatures.[10]

---

1 John 1:2-3; Hebrews 1:2; Job 26:13 **2** Romans 1:20 **3** Colossians 1:16; Genesis 1:31 **4** Genesis 1:27 **5** Genesis 2:7 **6** Ecclesiastes 7:29; Genesis 1:26 **7** Romans 2:14-15 **8** Genesis 3:6 **9** Genesis 2:17 **10** Genesis 1:26,28

CHAPTER 5
DIVINE PROVIDENCE

1. God the good Creator of all things, in His infinite power and wisdom does uphold, direct, dispose, and govern all creatures and things,[1] from the greatest even to the least,[2] by His most wise and holy providence, to the end for the which they were created, according unto His infallible foreknowledge, and the free and immutable counsel of His own will; to the praise of the glory of His wisdom, power, justice, infinite goodness, and mercy.[3]

2. Although in relation to the foreknowledge and decree of God, the first cause, all things come to pass immutably and infallibly;[4] so that there is not anything befalls any by chance, or without His providence;[5] yet by the same providence He ordered them to fall out according to the nature of second causes, either necessarily, freely, or contingently.[6]

3. God, in his ordinary providence makes use of means,[7] yet is free to work without,[8] above,[9] and against them[10] at His pleasure.

4. The almighty power, unsearchable wisdom, and infinite goodness of God, so far manifest themselves in His providence, that His determinate counsel extends itself even to the first fall, and all other sinful actions both of angels and men;[11] and that not by a bare permission, which also He most wisely and powerfully binds, and otherwise orders and governs,[12] in a

manifold dispensation to His most holy ends;[13] yet so, as the sinfulness of their acts proceeds only from the creatures, and not from God, who, being most holy and righteous, neither is nor can be the author or approver of sin.[14]

5. The most wise, righteous, and gracious God does often times leave for a season His own children to manifold temptations and the corruptions of their own hearts, to chastise them for their former sins, or to discover unto them the hidden strength of corruption and deceitfulness of their hearts, that they may be humbled; and to raise them to a more close and constant dependence for their support upon Himself; and to make them more watchful against all future occasions of sin, and for other just and holy ends.[15] So that whatsoever befalls any of His elect is by His appointment, for His glory, and their good.[16]

6. As for those wicked and ungodly men whom God, as the righteous judge, for former sin does blind and harden;[17] from them He not only withholds His grace, whereby they might have been enlightened in their understanding, and wrought upon their hearts;[18] but sometimes also withdraws the gifts which they had,[19] and exposes them to such objects as their corruption makes occasion of sin;[20] and withal, gives them over to their own lusts, the temptations of the world, and the power of Satan,[21] whereby it comes to pass that they harden themselves, under those means which God uses for the softening of others.[22]

7. As the providence of God does in general reach to all creatures, so after a more special manner it takes care of His church, and disposes of all things to the good thereof.[23]

1 Hebrews 1:3; Job 38:11; Isaiah 46:10-11; Psalm 135:6 **2** Matthew 10:29-31
3 Ephesians 1:11 **4** Acts 2:23 **5** Proverbs 16:33 **6** Genesis 8:22 **7** Acts 27:31, 44;
Isaiah 55:10-11 **8** Hosea 1:7 **9** Rom. 4:19-21 **10** Dan. 3:27 **11** Romans 11:32-34;
2 Samuel 24:1; 1 Chronicles 21:1 **12** 2 Kings 19:28; Psalm 76:10 **13** Genesis 1:20;
Isaiah 10:6-7,12 **14** Psalm 50:21; 1 John 2:16 **15** 2 Chronicles 32:25-26,31;
2 Corinthians 12:7-9 **16** Romans 8:28 **17** Romans 1:24-26,28, 11:7,8
18 Deuteronomy 29:4 **19** Matthew 13:12 **20** Deuteronomy 2:30; 2 Kings 8:12-13 **21** Psalm 81:11-12; 2 Thessalonians 2:10-12 **22** Exodus 8:15,32; Isaiah 6:9-10;
1 Peter 2:7-8 23 1 Timothy 4:10; Amos 9:8-9; Isaiah 43:3-5 **23** 1 Timothy 4:10; Amos 9:8-9; Isaiah 43:3-5

CHAPTER 6:
THE FALL OF MAN, SIN, & ITS PUNISHMENT

1. Although God created man upright and perfect, and gave him a righteous law, which had been unto life had he kept it, and threatened death upon the breach thereof,[1] yet he did not long abide in this honor; Satan using the subtlety of the serpent to subdue Eve, then by her seducing Adam, who, without any compulsion, did willfully transgress the law of their creation, and the command given to them, in eating the forbidden fruit,[2] which God was pleased, according to His wise and holy counsel to permit, having purposed to order it to His own glory.

2. Our first parents, by this sin, fell from their original righteousness and communion with God, and we in them whereby death came upon all:[3] all becoming dead in sin,[4] and wholly defiled in all the faculties and parts of soul and body.[5]

3. They being the root, and by God's appointment, standing in the room and stead of all mankind, the guilt of the sin was imputed, and corrupted nature conveyed, to all their posterity descending from them by ordinary generation,[6] being now conceived in sin,[7] and by nature children of wrath,[8] the servants of sin, the subjects of death,[9] and all other miseries, spiritual, temporal, and eternal, unless the Lord Jesus set them free.[10]

4. From this original corruption, whereby we are utterly indisposed, disabled, and made opposite to all good, and wholly inclined to all evil,[11] do proceed all actual transgressions.[12]

5. The corruption of nature, during this life, does remain in those that are regenerated;[13] and although it be through Christ pardoned and mortified, yet both itself, and the first motions thereof, are truly and properly sin.[14]

---

[1] Genesis 2:16-17 [2] Genesis 3:12-13; 2 Corinthians 11:3 [3] Romans 3:23
[4] Romans 5:12, etc. [5] Titus 1:15; Genesis 6:5; Jeremiah 17:9; Rom. 3:10-19
[6] Romans 5:12-19; 1 Corinthians 15:21-22,45,49 [7] Psalm 51:5; Job 14:4
[8] Ephesians 2:3 [9] Romans 6:20, 5:12 [10] Hebrews 2:14-15; 1 Thessalonians 1:10
[11] Romans 8:7; Colossians 1:21 [12] James 1:14-15; Matthew 15:19
[13] Romans 7:18,23; Ecclesiastes 7:20; 1 John 1:8 [14] Romans 7:23-25; Galatians 5:17

CHAPTER 7:
GOD'S COVENANT

1. The distance between God and the creature is so great, that although reasonable creatures do owe obedience to Him as their creator, yet they could never have attained the reward of life but by some voluntary condescension on God's part, which He hath been pleased to express by way of covenant.[1]

2. Moreover, man having brought himself under the curse of the law by his fall, it pleased the Lord to make a covenant of grace,[2] wherein He freely offers unto sinners life and salvation by Jesus Christ, requiring of them faith in Him, that they may be saved;[3] and promising to give unto all those that are ordained unto eternal life, His Holy Spirit, to make them willing and able to believe.[4]

3. This covenant is revealed in the gospel; first of all to Adam in the promise of salvation by the seed of the woman,[5] and afterwards by farther steps, until the full discovery thereof was completed in the New Testament;[6] and it is founded in that eternal covenant transaction that was between the Father and the Son about the redemption of the elect;[7] and it is alone by the grace of this covenant that all the posterity of fallen Adam that ever were saved did obtain life and blessed immortality, man being now utterly incapable of acceptance with God upon those terms on which Adam stood in his state of innocency.[8]

1 Luke 17:10; Job 35:7-8 **2** Genesis 2:17; Galatians 3:10; Romans 3:20-21
3 Romans 8:3; Mark 16:15-16; John 3:16 **4** Ezekiel 36:26-27; John 6:44-45;
Psalm 110:3 **5** Genesis 3:15 **6** Hebrews 1:1 **7** 2 Timothy 1:9; Titus 1:2
8 Hebrews 11:6,13; Romans 4:1-2, etc.; Acts 4:12; John 8:56

CHAPTER 8:
CHRIST THE MEDIATOR

1. It pleased God, in His eternal purpose, to choose and ordain the Lord Jesus, His only begotten Son, according to the covenant made between them both, to be the mediator between God and man;[1] the prophet,[2] priest,[3] and king;[4] head and savior of the church,[5] the heir of all things,[6] and judge of the world;[7] unto whom He did from all eternity give a people to be His seed and to be by Him in time redeemed, called, justified, sanctified, and glorified.[8]

2. The Son of God, the second person in the Holy Trinity, being very and eternal God, the brightness of the Father's glory, of one substance and equal with Him who made the world, who upholds and governs all things He has made, did, when the fullness of time was complete, take upon Him man's nature, with all the essential properties and common infirmities of it,[9] yet without sin;[10] being conceived by the Holy Spirit in the womb of the Virgin Mary, the Holy Spirit coming down upon her: and the power of the Most High overshadowing her; and so was made of a woman of the tribe of Judah, of the seed of Abraham and David according to the Scriptures;[11] so that two whole, perfect, and distinct natures were inseparably joined together in one person, without conversion, composition, or confusion; which person is very God and very man, yet one Christ, the only mediator between God and man.[12]

3. The Lord Jesus, in His human nature thus united to the divine, in the person of the Son, was sanctified and anointed with the Holy Spirit above measure,[13] having in Him all the treasures of wisdom and knowledge;[14] in whom it pleased the Father that all fullness should dwell,[15] to the end that being holy, harmless, undefiled,[16] and full of grace and truth,[17] He might be thoroughly furnished to execute the office of mediator and surety;[18] which office He took not upon himself, but was thereunto called by His Father;[19] who also put all power and judgement in His hand, and gave Him commandment to execute the same.[20]

4. This office the Lord Jesus did most willingly undertake,[21] which that He might discharge He was made under the law,[22] and did perfectly fulfill it, and underwent the punishment due to us, which we should have borne and suffered,[23] being made sin and a curse for us;[24] enduring most grievous sorrows in His soul, and most painful sufferings in His body;[25] was crucified, and died, and remained in the state of the dead, yet saw no corruption:[26] on the third day He arose from the dead[27] with the same body in which He suffered,[28] with which He also ascended into heaven,[29] and there sits at the right hand of His Father making intercession,[30] and shall return to judge men and angels at the end of the world.[31]

5. The Lord Jesus, by His perfect obedience and sacrifice of Himself, which He through the eternal Spirit once offered up to God, has fully satisfied the justice of God,[32] procured reconciliation, and purchased an everlasting inheritance in the kingdom of heaven, for all those whom the Father has given unto Him.[33]

6. Although the price of redemption was not actually paid by Christ until after His incarnation, yet the virtue, efficacy, and benefit thereof were communicated to the elect in all ages, successively from the beginning of the world, in and by those promises, types, and sacrifices wherein He was revealed, and signified to be the seed which should bruise the serpent's head;[34] and the Lamb slain from the foundation of the world,[35] being the same yesterday, and today and for ever.[36]

7. Christ, in the work of mediation, acts according to both natures, by each nature doing that which is proper to itself; yet by reason of the unity of the person, that which is proper to one nature is sometimes in Scripture, attributed to the person denominated by the other nature.[37]

8. To all those for whom Christ has obtained eternal redemption, He does certainly and effectually apply and communicate the same, making intercession for them;[38] uniting them to Himself by His Spirit, revealing to them, in and by His Word, the mystery of salvation, persuading them to believe and obey,[39] governing their hearts by His Word and Spirit,[40] and overcoming all their enemies by His almighty power and wisdom,[41] in such manner and ways as are most consonant to His wonderful and unsearchable dispensation; and all of free and absolute grace, without any condition foreseen in them to procure it.[42]

9. This office of mediator between God and man is proper only to Christ, who is the prophet, priest, and king of the church of God; and may not be either in whole, or any part thereof, transferred from Him to any other.[43]

10. This number and order of offices is necessary; for in respect of our ignorance, we stand in need of His prophetical office;[44]

and in respect of our alienation from God, and imperfection of the best of our services, we need His priestly office to reconcile us and present us acceptable unto God;[45] and in respect to our averseness and utter inability to return to God, and for our rescue and security from our spiritual adversaries, we need His kingly office to convince, subdue, draw, uphold, deliver, and preserve us to His heavenly kingdom.[46]

---

1 Isaiah 42:1; 1 Peter 1:19-20 **2** Acts 3:22 **3** Hebrews 5:5-6 **4** Psalm 2:6; Luke 1:33 **5** Ephesians 1:22-23 **6** Hebrews 1:2 **7** Acts 17:31 **8** Isaiah 53:10; John 17:6; Romans 8:30 **9** John 1:14; Galatians 4:4 **10** Romans 8:3; Hebrews 2:14,16-17, 4:15 **11** Matthew 1:22-23 **12** Luke 1:27,31,35; Romans 9:5; 1 Timothy 2:5 **13** Psalm 45:7; Acts 10:38; John 3:34 **14** Colossians 2:3 **15** Colossians 1:19 **16** Hebrews 7:26 **17** John 1:14 **18** Hebrews 7:22 **19** Hebrews 5:5 **20** John 5:22,27; Matthew 28:18; Acts 2:36 **21** Psalm 40:7-8; Hebrews 10:5-10; John 10:18 **22** Galatians 4:4; Matthew 3:15 **23** Galatians 3:13; Isaiah 53:6; 1 Peter 3:18 **24** 2 Corinthians 5:21 **25** Matthew 26:37-38; Luke 22:44; Matthew 27:46 **26** Acts 13:37 **27** 1 Corinthians 15:3-4 **28** John 20:25,27 **29** Mark 16:19; Acts 1:9-11 **30** Romans 8:34; Hebrews 9:24 **31** Acts 10:42; Romans 14:9-10; Acts 1:11; 2 Peter 2:4 **32** Hebrews 9:14, 10:14; Romans 3:25-26 **33** John 17:2; Hebrews 9:15 **34** 1 Corinthians 4:10; Hebrews 4:2; 1 Peter 1:10-11 **35** Revelation 13:8 **36** Hebrews 13:8 **37** John 3:13; Acts 20:28 **38** John 6:37, 10:15-16, 17:9; Romans 5:10 **39** John 17:6; Ephesians 1:9; 1 John 5:20 **40** Romans 8:9,14 **41** Psalm 110:1; 1 Corinthians 15:25-26 **42** John 3:8; Ephesians 1:8 **43** 1 Timothy 2:5 **44** John 1:18 **45** Colossians 1:21; Galatians 5:17 **46** John 16:8; Psalm 110:3; Luke 1:74-75

CHAPTER 9:
FREE WILL

1. God has endued the will of man with that natural liberty and power of acting upon choice, that it is neither forced, nor by any necessity of nature determined to do good or evil.[1]

2. Man, in his state of innocency, had freedom and power to will and to do that which was good and well-pleasing to God,[2] but yet was unstable, so that he might fall from it.[3]

3. Man, by his fall into a state of sin, has wholly lost all ability of will to any spiritual good accompanying salvation;[4] so as a natural man, being altogether averse from that good, and dead in sin,[5] is not able by his own strength to convert himself, or to prepare himself thereunto.[6]

4. When God converts a sinner, and translates him into the state of grace, He frees him from his natural bondage under sin,[7] and by His grace alone enables him freely to will and to do that which is spiritually good;[8] yet so as that by reason of his remaining corruptions, he does not perfectly, nor only will, that which is good, but does also will that which is evil.[9]

5. This will of man is made perfectly and immutably free to good alone in the state of glory only.[10]

---

[1] Matthew 17:12; James 1:14; Deuteronomy 30:19 [2] Ecclesiastes 7:29
[3] Genesis 3:6 [4] Romans 5:6, 8:7 [5] Ephesians 2:1,5 [6] Titus 3:3-5; John 6:44
[7] Colossians 1:13; John 8:36 [8] Philippians 2:13 [9] Romans 7:15,18-19,21,23
[10] Ephesians 4:13

CHAPTER 10:
EFFECTUAL CALLING

1. Those whom God hath predestined unto life, He is pleased in His appointed, and accepted time, effectually to call,[1] by His Word and Spirit, out of that state of sin and death in which they are by nature, to grace and salvation by Jesus Christ;[2] enlightening their minds spiritually and savingly to understand the things of God;[3] taking away their heart of stone, and giving to them a heart of flesh;[4] renewing their wills, and by His almighty power determining them to that which is good, and effectually drawing them to Jesus Christ;[5] yet so as they come most freely, being made willing by His grace.[6]

2. This effectual call is of God's free and special grace alone, not from anything at all foreseen in man, nor from any power or agency in the creature,[7] being wholly passive therein, being dead in sins and trespasses, until being quickened and renewed by the Holy Spirit;[8] he is thereby enabled to answer this call, and to embrace the grace offered and conveyed in it, and that by no less power than that which raised up Christ from the dead.[9]

3. Elect infants dying in infancy are regenerated and saved by Christ through the Spirit;[10] who works when, and where, and how He pleases;[11] so also are all elect persons, who are incapable of being outwardly called by the ministry of the Word. (see note at the end of chapter 10)

4. Others not elected, although they may be called by the ministry of the Word, and may have some common operations of the Spirit,[12] yet not being effectually drawn by the Father, they neither will nor can truly come to Christ, and therefore cannot be saved:[13] much less can men that do not receive the Christian religion be saved; be they never so diligent to frame their lives according to the light of nature and the law of that religion they do profess.[14]

(Chapter 10, paragraph 3 speaks of elect infants dying in infancy. The topic is a challenging one theologically and pastorally and should be approached with maturity. May the Lord grant maturity beyond our natural years! While history is not the authority, an awareness of the commonly held convictions of those of like precious faith should give us reason for pause at the very least. These men were considered strict Baptists whose theology was anything but soft.)

---

1 Romans 8:30, 11:7; Ephesians 1:10-11; 2 Thessalonians 2:13-14 **2** Ephesians 2:1-6 **3** Acts 26:18; Ephesians 1:17-18 **4** Ezekiel 36:26 **5** Deuteronomy 30:6; Ezekiel 36:27; Ephesians 1:19 **6** Psalm 110:3; Song of Solomon 1:4 **7** 2 Timothy 1:9; Ephesians 2:8 **8** 1 Corinthians 2:14; Ephesians 2:5; John 5:25 **9** Ephesians 1:19-20 **10** John 3:3-6 **11** John 3:8 **12** Matthew 22:14, 13:20-21; Hebrews 6:4-5 **13** John 6:44-45,65; 1 John 2:24-25 **14** Acts 4:12; John 4:22, 17:3

CHAPTER 11: JUSTIFICATION

1. Those whom God effectually calls, he also freely justifies,[1] not by infusing righteousness into them, but by pardoning their sins, and by accounting and accepting their persons as righteous;[2] not for anything wrought in them, or done by them, but for Christ's sake alone;[3] not by imputing faith itself, the act of believing, or any other evangelical obedience to them, as their righteousness; but by imputing Christ's active obedience unto the whole law, and passive obedience in his death for their whole and sole righteousness by faith,[4] which faith they have not of themselves; it is the gift of God.[5]

2. Faith thus receiving and resting on Christ and his righteousness, is the alone instrument of justification;[6] yet is not alone in the person justified, but is ever accompanied with all other saving graces, and is no dead faith, but works by love.[7]

3. Christ, by his obedience and death, did fully discharge the debt of all those who are justified; and did, by the sacrifice of himself in the blood of his cross, undergoing in their stead the penalty due to them, make a proper, real, and full satisfaction to God's justice in their behalf;[8] yet, in as much as he was given by the Father for them, and his obedience and satisfaction accepted in their stead, and both freely, not for anything in them,[9] their justification is only of free grace, that both the exact justice and rich grace of God might be glorified in the justification of sinners.[10]

4. God did from all eternity decree to justify all the elect,[11] and Christ did in the fullness of time die for their sins, and rise again for their justification;[12] nevertheless, they are not justified personally, until the Holy Spirit in time does actually apply Christ to them.[13]

5. God continues to forgive the sins of those that are justified,[14] and although they can never fall from the state of justification,[15] yet they may, by their sins, fall under God's fatherly displeasure;16 and in that condition they usually do not have the light of his countenance restored to them, until they humble themselves, beg pardon, and renew their faith and repentance.[17]

6. The justification of believers under the Old Testament was, in all these respects, one and the same with the justification of believers under the New Testament.[18]

---

1 Romans 3:24, 8:30 **2** Romans 4:5-8, Ephesians 1:7 **3** 1 Corinthians 1:30,31, Romans 5:17-19 **4** Philippians 3:8,9; Ephesians 2:8-10 **5** John 1:12, Romans 5:17 **6** Romans 3:28 **7** Galatians 5:6, James 2:17,22,26 **8** Hebrews 10:14; 1 Peter 1:18-19; Isaiah 53:5-6 **9** Romans 8:32; 2 Corinthians 5:21 **10** Romans 3:26; Ephesians 1:6-7, 2:7 **11** Galatians 3:8; 1 Peter 1:2; 1 Timothy 2:6 **12** Romans 4:25 **13** Colossians 1:21-22; Titus 3:4-7 **14** Matthew 6:12; 1 John 1:7,9 **15** John 10:28 **16** Psalm 89:31-33 **17** Psalm 32:5; Psalm 51; Matthew 26:75 **18** Galatians 3:9; Rom. 4:22-24

CHAPTER 12:
ADOPTION

1. All those that are justified, God conferred, in and for the sake of his only Son Jesus Christ, to make partakers of the grace of adoption,[1] by which they are taken into the number, and enjoy the liberties and privileges of the children of God,[2] have his name put on them,[3] receive the spirit of adoption,[4] have access to the throne of grace with boldness, are enabled to cry Abba, Father,[5] are pitied,[6] protected,[7] provided for,[8] and chastened by him as by a Father,[9] yet never cast off,[10] but sealed to the day of redemption,[11] and inherit the promises as heirs of everlasting salvation.[12]

---

[1] Ephesians 1:5; Galatians 4:4-5 [2] John 1:12; Romans 8:17 [3] 2 Corinthians 6:18; Revelation 3:12 [4] Romans 8:15 [5] Galatians 4:6; Ephesians 2:18 [6] Psalm 103:13 [7] Proverbs 14:26 [8] 1 Peter 5:7 [9] Hebrews 12:6 [10] Isaiah 54:8-9; Lamentations 3:31 [11] Ephesians 4:30 [12] Hebrews 1:14, 6:12

CHAPTER 13:
SANCTIFICATION

1. They who are united to Christ, effectually called, and regenerated, having a new heart and a new spirit created in them through the virtue of Christ's death and resurrection, are also farther sanctified, really and personally,[1] through the same virtue, by his Word and Spirit dwelling in them;[2] the dominion of the whole body of sin is destroyed,[3] and the several lusts of it are more and more weakened and mortified,[4] and they more and more quickened and strengthened in all saving graces,[5] to the practice of all true holiness, without which no man shall see the Lord.[6]

2. This sanctification is throughout the whole man,[7] yet imperfect in this life; there abides still some remnants of corruption in every part,[8] wherefrom arises a continual and irreconcilable war; the flesh lusting against the Spirit, and the Spirit against the flesh.[9]

3. In which war, although the remaining corruption for a time may much prevail,[10] yet, through the continual supply of strength from the sanctifying Spirit of Christ, the regenerate part does overcome;[11] and so the saints grow in grace, perfecting holiness in the fear of God, pressing after an heavenly life, in evangelical obedience to all the commands which Christ as Head and King, in his Word has prescribed to them.[12]

1 Acts 20:32; Romans 6:5-6 **2** John 17:17; Ephesians 3:16-19; 1 Thessalonians 5:21-23 **3** Romans 6:14 **4** Galatians 5:24 **5** Colossians 1:11 **6** 2 Corinthians 7:1; Hebrews 12:14 **7** 1 Thessalonians 5:23 **8** Romans 7:18,23 **9** Galatians 5:17; 1 Peter 2:11 **10** Romans 7:23 **11** Romans 6:14 **12** Ephesians 4:15-16; 2 Corinthians 3:18, 7:1

CHAPTER 14:
SAVING FAITH

1. The grace of faith, whereby the elect are enabled to believe to the saving of their souls, is the work of the Spirit of Christ in their hearts,[1] and is ordinarily wrought by the ministry of the Word;[2] by which also, and by the administration of baptism and the Lord's supper, prayer, and other means appointed of God, it is increased and strengthened.[3]

2. By this faith a Christian believes to be true whatsoever is revealed in the Word for the authority of God himself,[4] and also apprehends an excellency therein above all other writings and all things in the world,[5] as it bears forth the glory of God in his attributes, the excellency of Christ in his nature and offices, and the power and fullness of the Holy Spirit in his workings and operations: and so is enabled to cast his soul upon the truth consequently believed;[6] and also acts differently upon that which each particular passage thereof contains; yielding obedience to the commands,[7] trembling at the threatenings,[8] and embracing the promises of God for this life and that which is to come;[9] but the principle acts of saving faith have immediate relation to Christ, accepting, receiving, and resting upon him alone for justification, sanctification, and eternal life, by virtue of the covenant of grace.[10]

3. This faith, although it be in different stages, and may be weak or strong,[11] yet it is in the least degree of it different in the kind or nature of it, as is all other saving grace, from the faith and

common grace of temporary believers;[12] and therefore, though it may be many times assailed and weakened, yet it gets the victory,[13] growing up in many to the attainment of a full assurance through Christ,[14] who is both the author and finisher of our faith.[15]

---

1 2 Corinthians 4:13; Ephesians 2:8 **2** Romans 10:14,17 **3** Luke 17:5; 1 Peter 2:2; Acts 20:32 **4** Acts 24:14 **5** Psalm 19:7-10, 119:72 **6** 2 Timothy 1:12 **7** John 15:14 **8** Isaiah 66:2 **9** Hebrews 11:13 **10** John 1:12; Acts 16:31; Galatians 2:20; Acts 15:11 **11** Hebrews 5:13-14; Matthew 6:30; Romans 4:19-20 **12** 2 Peter 1:1 **13** Ephesians 6:16; 1 John 5:4-5 **14** Hebrews 6:11-12; Colossians 2:2 **15** Hebrews 12:2

CHAPTER 15:
REPENTANCE & SALVATION

1. Such of the elect that are converted at riper years, having sometime lived in the state of nature, and therein served divers pleasures, God in their effectual calling gives them repentance to life.[1]

2. Whereas there is none that does good and does not sin,[2] and the best of men may, through the power and deceitfulness of their corruption dwelling in them, with the prevalence of temptation, fall in to great sins and provocations; God has, in the covenant of grace, mercifully provided that believers so sinning and falling be renewed through repentance unto salvation.[3]

3. This saving repentance is an evangelical grace,[4] whereby a person, being by the Holy Spirit made sensible of the manifold evils of his sin, does, by faith in Christ, humble himself for it with godly sorrow, detestation of it, and self-abhorrancy,[5] praying for pardon and strength of grace, with a purpose and endeavor, by supplies of the Spirit, to walk before God unto all well-pleasing in all things.[6]

4. As repentance is to be continued through the whole course of our lives, upon the account of the body of death, and the motions thereof, so it is every man's duty to repent of his particular known sins particularly.[7]

5. Such is the provision which God has made through Christ in the covenant of grace for the preservation of believers unto salvation, that although there is no sin so small but it deserves damnation,[8] yet there is no sin so great that it shall bring damnation to them that repent,[9] which makes the constant preaching of repentance necessary.

---

[1] Titus 3:2-5 [2] Ecclesiastes 7:20 [3] Luke 22:31-32 [4] Zechariah 12:10; Acts 11:18 [5] Ezekiel 36:31; 2 Corinthians 7:11 [6] Psalm 119:6,128 [7] Luke 19:8; 1 Timothy 1:13,15 [8] Romans 6:23 [9] Isaiah 1:16-18, 55:7

CHAPTER 16:
GOOD WORKS

1. Good works are only such as God has commanded in his Holy Word,[1] and not such as without the warrant thereof are devised by men out of blind zeal, or upon any pretense of good intentions.[2]

2. These good works, done in obedience to God's commandments, are the fruits and evidences of a true and lively faith;[3] and by them believers manifest their thankfulness,[4] strengthen their assurance,[5] edify their brethren, adorn the profession of the gospel,[6] stop the mouths of the adversaries, and glorify God[7], whose workmanship they are, created in Christ Jesus thereunto,[8] that having their fruit unto holiness they may have the end eternal life.[9]

3. Their ability to do good works is not all of themselves, but wholly from the Spirit of Christ;[10] and that they may be enabled thereunto, besides the graces they have already received, there is necessary an actual influence of the same Holy Spirit, to work in them and to will and to do of his good pleasure;[11] yet they are not bound to perform any duty, unless upon a special motion of the Spirit, but they ought to be diligent in stirring up the grace of God that is in them.[12]

4. They who in their obedience attain to the greatest height which is possible in this life, are so far from being able to supererogate, and to do more than God requires, as that they fall short of much which in duty they are bound to do.[13]

5. We cannot by our best works merit pardon of sin or eternal life at the hand of God, by reason of the great disproportion that is between them and the glory to come, and the infinite distance that is between us and God, whom by them we can neither profit nor satisfy for the debt of our former sins;[14] but when we have done all we can, we have done but our duty, and are unprofitable servants; and because they are good they proceed from his Spirit,[15] and as they are wrought by us they are defiled and mixed with so much weakness and imperfection, that they cannot endure the severity of God's punishment.[16]

6. Yet notwithstanding the persons of believers being accepted through Christ, their good works also are accepted in him;[17] not as though they were in this life wholly unblamable and unreprovable in God's sight, but that he, looking upon them in his Son, is pleased to accept and reward that which is sincere, although accompanied with many weaknesses and imperfection.[18]

7. Works done by unregenerate men, although for the matter of them they may be things which God commands, and of good use both to themselves and to others;[19] yet because they proceed not from a heart purified by faith,[20] nor are done in a right manner according to the Word,[21] nor to a right end, the glory of God,[22] they are therefore sinful, and cannot please God, nor make a man meet to receive the grace from God,[23] and yet their neglect for them is more sinful and displeasing to God.[24]

---

1 Micah 6:8; Hebrews 13:21 **2** Matthew 15:9; Isaiah 29:13 **3** James 2:18,22 **4** Psalm 116:12-13 **5** 1 John 2:3,5; 2 Peter 1:5-11 **6** Matthew 5:16 **7** 1 Timothy 6:1; 1 Peter 2:15; Philippians 1:11 **8** Ephesians 2:10 **9** Romans 6:22 **10** John 15:4-5 **11** 2 Corinthians 3:5; Philippians 2:13 **12** Philippians 2:12; Hebrews 6:11-12; Isaiah 64:7 **13** Job 9:2-3; Galatians 5:17; Luke 17:10 **14** Romans 3:20;

Ephesians 2:8-9; Romans 4:6 **15** Galatians 5:22-23 **16** Isaiah 64:6; Psalm 43:2 **17** Ephesians 1:5; 1 Peter 1:5 **18** Matthew 25:21,23; Hebrews 6:10 **19** 2 Kings 10:30; 1 Kings 21:27,29 **20** Genesis 4:5; Hebrews 11:4,6 **21** 1 Corinthians 13:1 **22** Matthew 6:2,5 **23** Amos 5:21-22; Romans 9:16; Titus 3:5 **24** Job 21:14-15; Matthew 25:41-43

CHAPTER 17:
THE PERSEVERANCE OF THE SAINTS

1. Those whom God has accepted in the beloved, effectually called and sanctified by his Spirit, and given the precious faith of his elect unto, can neither totally nor finally fall from the state of grace, but shall certainly persevere therein to the end, and be eternally saved, seeing the gifts and callings of God are without repentance, from which source he still begets and nourishes in them faith, repentance, love, joy, hope, and all the graces of the Spirit unto immortality;[1] and though many storms and floods arise and beat against them, yet they shall never be able to take them off that foundation and rock which by faith they are fastened upon; notwithstanding, through unbelief and the temptations of Satan, the sensible sight of the light and love of God may for a time be clouded and obscured from them,[2] yet he is still the same, and they shall be sure to be kept by the power of God unto salvation, where they shall enjoy their purchased possession, they being engraved upon the palm of his hands, and their names having been written in the book of life from all eternity.[3]

2. This perseverance of the saints depends not upon their own free will, but upon the immutability of the decree of election,[4] flowing from the free and unchangeable love of God the Father, upon the efficacy of the merit and intercession of Jesus Christ and union with him,[5] the oath of God,[6] the abiding of his

Spirit, and the seed of God within them,[7] and the nature of the covenant of grace;[8] from all which ariseth also the certainty and infallibility thereof.

3. And though they may, through the temptation of Satan and of the world, the prevalency of corruption remaining in them, and the neglect of means of their preservation, fall into grievous sins, and for a time continue therein,[9] whereby they incur God's displeasure and grieve his Holy Spirit,[10] come to have their graces and comforts impaired,[11] have their hearts hardened, and their consciences wounded,[12] hurt and scandalize others, and bring temporal judgments upon themselves,[13] yet shall they renew their repentance and be preserved through faith in Christ Jesus to the end.[14]

---

1 John 10:28-29; Philippians 1:6; 2 Timothy 2:19; 1 John 2:19 **2** Psalm 89:31-32; 1 Corinthians 11:32 **3** Malachi 3:6 **4** Romans 8:30, 9:11,16 **5** Romans 5:9-10; John 14:19 **6** Hebrews 6:17-18 **7** 1 John 3:9 **8** Jeremiah 32:40 **9** Matthew 26:70,72,74 **10** Isaiah 64:5,9; Ephesians 4:30 **11** Psalm 51:10,12 **12** Psalm 32:3-4 **13** 2 Samuel 12:14 **14** Luke 22:32,61-62

CHAPTER 18:
ASSURANCE OF SALVATION

1. Although temporary believers and other unregenerate men, may vainly deceive themselves with false hopes and carnal presumptions of being in the favor of God and in a state of salvation, which hope of theirs shall perish;[1] yet such as truly believe in the Lord Jesus, and love him in sincerity, endeavoring to walk in all good conscience before him, may in this life be certainly assured that they are in the state of grace, and may rejoice in the hope of the glory of God,[2] which hope shall never make them ashamed.[3]

2. This certainty is not a bare conjectural and probable persuasion grounded upon a fallible hope, but an infallible assurance of faith,[4] founded on the blood and righteousness of Christ revealed in the Gospel;[5] and also upon the inward evidence of those graces of the Spirit unto which promises are made,[6] and on the testimony of the Spirit of adoption, witnessing with our spirits that we are the children of God;[7] and, as a fruit thereof, keeping the heart both humble and holy.[8]

3. This infallible assurance does not so belong to the essence of faith, but that a true believer may wait long, and struggle with many difficulties before he be partaker of it;[9] yet being enabled by the Spirit to know the things which are freely given him of God, he may, without extraordinary revelation, in the right use of means, attain thereunto:[10] and therefore it is the duty of every one to give all diligence to make his calling and

election sure, that thereby his heart may be enlarged in peace and joy in the Holy Spirit, in love and thankfulness to God, and in strength and cheerfulness in the duties of obedience, the proper fruits of this assurance;[11] -so far is it from inclining men to looseness.[12]

4. True believers may have the assurance of their salvation divers ways shaken, diminished, and intermitted; as by negligence in preserving of it,[13] by falling into some special sin which wounds the conscience and grieves the Spirit;[14] by some sudden or vehement temptation,[15] by God's withdrawing the light of his countenance, and suffering even such as fear him to walk in darkness and to have no light,[16] yet are they never destitute of the seed of God[17] and life of faith,[18] that love of Christ and the brethren, that sincerity of heart and conscience of duty out of which, by the operation of the Spirit, this assurance may in due time be revived,[19] and by the which, in the meantime, they are preserved from utter despair.[20]

---

[1] Job 8:13-14; Matthew 7:22-23 [2] 1 John 2:3, 3:14,18-19,21,24, 5:13 [3] Romans 5:2,5 [4] Hebrews 6:11,19 [5] Hebrews 6:17-18 [6] 2 Peter 1:4-5,10-11 [7] Romans 8:15-16 [8] 1 John 3:1-3 [9] Isaiah 50:10; Psalm 88; Psalm 77:1-12 [10] 1 John 4:13; Hebrews 6:11-12 [11] Romans 5:1,2,5, 14:17; Psalm 119:32 [12] Romans 6:1-2; Titus 2:11-12,14 [13] Song of Solomon 5:2-3,6 [14] Psalm 51:8,12,14 [15] Psalm 116:11; 77:7-8; 31:22 [16] Psalm 30:7 [17] 1 John 3:9 [18] Luke 22:32 [19] Psalm 42:5,11 [20] Lamentations 3:26-31

CHAPTER 19:
THE LAW OF GOD

1. God gave to Adam a law of universal obedience written in his heart, and a particular precept of not eating the fruit of the tree of knowledge of good and evil;[1] by which he bound him and all his posterity to personal, entire, exact, and perpetual obedience;[2] promised life upon the fulfilling, and threatened death upon the breach of it, and endued him with power and ability to keep it.[3]

2. The same law that was first written in the heart of man continued to be a perfect rule of righteousness after the fall,[4] and was delivered by God upon Mount Sinai, in ten commandments, and written in two tables, the four first containing our duty towards God, and the other six, our duty to man.[5]

3. Besides this law, commonly called moral, God was pleased to give to the people of Israel ceremonial laws, containing several typical ordinances, partly of worship, prefiguring Christ, his graces, actions, sufferings, and benefits;[6] and partly holding forth divers instructions of moral duties,[7] all which ceremonial laws being appointed only to the time of reformation, are, by Jesus Christ the true Messiah and only law-giver, who was furnished with power from the Father for that end abrogated and taken away.[8]

4. To them also he gave sundry judicial laws, which expired together with the state of that people, not obliging any now by virtue of that institution; their general equity only being of modern use.[9]

5. The moral law does for ever bind all, as well justified persons as others, to the obedience thereof,[10] and that not only in regard of the matter contained in it, but also in respect of the authority of God the Creator, who gave it;[11] neither does Christ in the Gospel any way dissolve, but much strengthen this obligation.[12]

6. Although true believers are not under the law as a covenant of works, to be thereby justified or condemned,[13] yet it is of great use to them as well as to others, in that as a rule of life, informing them of the will of God and their duty, it directs and binds them to walk accordingly; discovering also the sinful pollutions of their natures, hearts, and lives, so as examining themselves thereby, they may come to further conviction of, humiliation for, and hatred against, sin;[14] together with a clearer sight of the need they have of Christ and the perfection of his obedience; it is likewise of use to the regenerate to restrain their corruptions, in that it forbids sin; and the threatenings of it serve to show what even their sins deserve, and what afflictions in this life they may expect for them, although freed from the curse and unallayed rigour thereof. The promises of it likewise show them God's approbation of obedience, and what blessings they may expect upon the performance thereof, though not as due to them by the law as a covenant of works; so as man's doing good and refraining from evil, because the law encourages to the one and deters from the other, is no evidence of his being under the law and not under grace.[15]

7. Neither are the aforementioned uses of the law contrary to the grace of the Gospel, but do sweetly comply with it,[16] the Spirit of Christ subduing and enabling the will of man to do that freely and cheerfully which the will of God, revealed in the law, requires to be done.[17]

1 Genesis 1:27; Ecclesiastes 7:29 **2** Romans 10:5 **3** Galatians 3:10,12 **4** Romans 2:14-15 **5** Deuteronomy 10:4 **6** Hebrews 10:1; Colossians 2:17 **7** 1 Corinthians 5:7 **8** Colossians 2:14,16-17; Ephesians 2:14,16 **9** 1 Corinthians 9:8-10 **10** Romans 13:8-10; James 2:8,10-12 **11** James 2:10-11 **12** Matthew 5:17-19; Romans 3:31 **13** Romans 6:14; Galatians 2:16; Romans 8:1,10:4 **14** Romans 3:20, 7:7, etc. **15** Romans 6:12-14; 1 Peter 3:8-13 **16** Galatians 3:21 **17** Ezekiel 36:27

CHAPTER 20:
THE GOSPEL & ITS INFLUENCE

1. The covenant of works being broken by sin, and made unprofitable unto life, God was pleased to give forth the promise of Christ, the seed of the woman, as the means of calling the elect, and begetting in them faith and repentance;[1] in this promise the gospel, as to the substance of it, was revealed, and [is] therein effectual for the conversion and salvation of sinners.[2]

2. This promise of Christ, and salvation by him, is revealed only by the Word of God;[3] neither do the works of creation or providence, with the light of nature, make discovery of Christ, or of grace by him, so much as in a general or obscure way;[4] much less that men destitute of the revelation of Him by the promise or gospel, should be enabled thereby to attain saving faith or repentance.[5]

3. The revelation of the gospel to sinners, made in divers times and by sundry parts, with the addition of promises and precepts for the obedience required therein, as to the nations and persons to whom it is granted, is merely of the sovereign will and good pleasure of God;[6] not being annexed by virtue of any promise to the due improvement of men's natural abilities, by virtue of common light received without it, which none ever made, or can do so;[7] and therefore in all ages, the preaching of

the gospel has been granted unto persons and nations, as to the extent or straitening of it, in great variety, according to the counsel of the will of God.

4. Although the gospel be the only outward means of revealing Christ and saving grace, and is, as such, abundantly sufficient thereunto; yet that men who are dead in trespasses may be born again, quickened or regenerated, there is moreover necessary an effectual insuperable work of the Holy Spirit upon the whole soul, for the producing in them a new spiritual life;[8] without which no other means will effect their conversion unto God.[9]

---

[1] Genesis 3:15 [2] Revelation 13:8 [3] Romans 1:17 [4] Romans 10:14-15,17
[5] Proverbs 29:18; Isaiah 25:7; 60:2-3 [6] Psalm 147:20; Acts 16:7
[7] Romans 1:18-32 [8] Psalm 110:3; 1 Corinthians 2:14; Ephesians 1:19-20
[9] John 6:44; 2 Corinthians 4:4,6

CHAPTER 21:

CHRISTIAN LIBERTY & LIBERTY OF CONSCIENCE

1. The liberty which Christ has purchased for believers under the gospel, consists in their freedom from the guilt of sin, the condemning wrath of God, the severity and curse of the law,[1] and in their being delivered from this present evil world,[2] bondage to Satan,[3] and dominion of sin,[4] from the evil of afflictions,[5] the fear and sting of death, the victory of the grave,[6] and everlasting damnation:[7] as also in their free access to God, and their yielding obedience unto Him, not out of slavish fear,[8] but a child-like love and willing mind.[9] All which were common also to believers under the law for the substance of them;[10] but under the New Testament the liberty of Christians is further enlarged, in their freedom from the yoke of a ceremonial law, to which the Jewish church was subjected, and in greater boldness of access to the throne of grace, and in fuller communications of the free Spirit of God, than believers under the law did ordinarily partake of.[11] (see note at the end of chapter 21)

2. God alone is Lord of the conscience,[12] and has left it free from the doctrines and commandments of men which are in any thing contrary to his word, or not contained in it.[13] So that to believe such doctrines, or obey such commands out of conscience, is to betray true liberty of conscience;[14] and the requiring of an implicit faith, an absolute and blind obedience, is to destroy liberty of conscience and reason also.[15]

3. They who upon pretense of Christian liberty do practice any sin, or cherish any sinful lust, as they do thereby pervert the main design of the grace of the gospel to their own destruction,[16] so they wholly destroy the end of Christian liberty, which is, that being delivered out of the hands of all our enemies, we might serve the Lord without fear, in holiness and righteousness before Him, all the days of our lives.[17]

---

1 Galatians 3:13 **2** Galatians 1:4 **3** Acts 26:18 **4** Romans 8:3 **5** Romans 8:28 **6** 1 Corinthians 15:54-57 **7** 2 Thessalonians 1:10 **8** Romans 8:15 **9** Luke 1:73-75; 1 John 4:18 **10** Galatians 3:9,14 **11** John 7:38-39; Hebrews 10:19-21 **12** James 4:12; Romans 14:4 **13** Acts 4:19,29; 1 Corinthians 7:23; Matthew 15:9 **14** Colossians 2:20,22-23 **15** 1 Corinthians 3:5; 2 Corinthians 1:24 **16** Romans 6:1-2 **17** Galatians 5:13; 2 Peter 2:18,21

(Chapter 21, paragraph 1 discusses the Christian's liberty from the ceremonial aspect of God's law. In doing so, the Old Testament saints are referred to as "the Jewish church." This is not a unique way of describing believers in the Old Testament as they were part of the believing assembly (ἐκκλησία/church in the Septuagint, e.g. Micah 2:5). But keep in mind that this is not how the New Testament ordinarily speaks of the church. In the New Testament the focus is the New Covenant Body of Christ comprised of both Jew and Gentile (Ephesians 2:16) established with the ascension of Christ and unique outpouring of His Spirit at Pentecost.)

CHAPTER 22:
WORSHIP & THE SABBATH DAY

1. The light of nature shows that there is a God, who has lordship and sovereignty over all; is just, good and does good to all; and is therefore to be feared, loved, praised, called upon, trusted in, and served, with all the heart and all the soul, and with all the might.[1] But the acceptable way of worshipping the true God, is instituted by himself,[2] and so limited by his own revealed will, that he may not be worshipped according to the imagination and devices of men, nor the suggestions of Satan, under any visible representations, or any other way not prescribed in the Holy Scriptures.[3]

2. Religious worship is to be given to God the Father, Son, and Holy Spirit, and to him alone;[4] not to angels, saints, or any other creatures;[5] and since the fall, not without a mediator,[6] nor in the mediation of any other but Christ alone.[7]

3. Prayer, with thanksgiving, being one part of natural worship, is by God required of all men.[8] But that it may be accepted, it is to be made in the name of the Son,[9] by the help of the Spirit,[10] according to his will;[11] with understanding, reverence, humility, fervency, faith, love, and perseverance; and when with others, in a known tongue.[12]

4. Prayer is to be made for things lawful, and for all sorts of men living, or that shall live hereafter;[13] but not for the dead,[14] nor for those of whom it may be known that they have sinned the sin unto death.[15]

5. The reading of the Scriptures,[16] preaching, and hearing the Word of God,[17] teaching and admonishing one another in psalms, hymns, and spiritual songs, singing with grace in our hearts to the Lord;[18] as also the administration of baptism,[19] and the Lord's supper,[20] are all parts of religious worship of God, to be performed in obedience to him, with understanding, faith, reverence, and godly fear; moreover, solemn humiliation, with fastings,[21] and thanksgivings, upon special occasions, ought to be used in an holy and religious manner.[22]

6. Neither prayer nor any other part of religious worship, is now under the gospel, tied unto, or made more acceptable by any place in which it is performed, or towards which it is directed; but God is to be worshipped everywhere in spirit and in truth;[23] as in private families[24] daily,[25] and in secret each one by himself;[26] so more solemnly in the public assemblies, which are not carelessly nor wilfully to be neglected or forsaken, when God by his word or providence calls thereunto.[27]

7. As it is the law of nature, that in general a proportion of time, by God's appointment, be set apart for the worship of God, so by his Word, in a positive moral, and perpetual commandment, binding all men, in all ages, he has particularly appointed one day in seven for a sabbath to be kept holy unto him,[28] which from the beginning of the world to the resurrection of Christ was the last day of the week, and from the resurrection of Christ was changed into the first day of the week, which is called the Lord's Day:[29] and is to be continued to the end of the

world as the Christian Sabbath, the observation of the last day of the week being abolished.

8. The sabbath is then kept holy unto the Lord, when men, after a due preparing of their hearts, and ordering their common affairs aforehand, do not only observe a holy rest all day, from their own works, words and thoughts, about their worldly employment and recreations,[30] but are also taken up the whole time in the public and private exercises of his worship, and in the duties of necessity and mercy.[31] (see note at the end of chapter 22)

(Chapter 22, paragraph 8 concerns "the Christian Sabbath." As was the common practice of the era and culture, the writers believed that Christians were obligated to keep the Sabbath, though on Sunday rather than Saturday. Therefore they discouraged everything from work to recreation. This is an issue where many have taken the approach that such are matters of conscience. We have not and do not plan on promoting a mandated Sabbath observance. Ultimately our Sabbath rest is in Christ (Hebrews 4:9; Matthew 11:28; Colossians 2:16-17).)

---

[1] Jeremiah 10:7; Mark 12:33 [2] Deuteronomy 12:32 [3] Exodus 20:4-6
[4] Matthew 4:9-10; John 6:23; Matthew 28:19 [5] Romans 1:25; Colossians 2:18; Revelation 19:10 [6] John 14:6 [7] 1 Timothy 2:5 [8] Psalm 95:1-7, 65:2
[9] John 14:13-14 [10] Rom. 8:26 [11] 1 John 5:14 [12] 1 Corinthians 14:16-17
[13] 1 Timothy 2:1-2; 2 Samuel 7:29 [14] 2 Samuel 12:21-23 [15] 1 John 5:16
[16] 1 Timothy 4:13 [17] 2 Timothy 4:2; Luke 8:18 [18] Colossians 3:16; Ephesians 5:19
[19] Matthew 28:19-20 [20] 1 Corinthians 11:26 [21] Esther 4:16; Joel 2:12
[22] Exodus 15:1-19, Psalm 107 [23] John 4:21; Malachi 1:11; 1 Timothy 2:8
[24] Acts 10:2 [25] Matthew 6:11; Psalm 55:17 [26] Matthew 6:6 [27] Hebrews 10:25; Acts 2:42 [28] Exodus 20:8 [29] 1 Corinthians 16:1-2; Acts 20:7; Revelation 1:10
[30] Isaiah 58:13; Nehemiah 13:15-22 [31] Matthew 12:1-13

CHAPTER 23:
LAWFUL OATHS & VOWS

1. A lawful oath is a part of religious worship, wherein the person swearing in truth, righteousness, and judgment, solemnly calls God to witness what he swears,[1] and to judge him according to the truth or falseness thereof.[2]

2. The name of God only is that by which men ought to swear; and therein it is to be used, with all holy fear and reverence; therefore to swear vainly or rashly by that glorious and dreadful name, or to swear at all by any other thing, is sinful, and to be abhorred;[3] yet as in matter of weight and moment, for confirmation of truth, and ending all strife, an oath is warranted by the word of God;[4] so a lawful oath being imposed by lawful authority in such matters, ought to be taken.[5]

3. Whosoever takes an oath warranted by the word of God, ought duly to consider the weightiness of so solemn an act, and therein to avouch nothing but what he knows to be truth; for that by rash, false, and vain oaths, the Lord is provoked, and for them this land mourns.[6]

4. An oath is to be taken in the plain and common sense of the words, without equivocation or mental reservation.[7]

5. A vow, which is not to be made to any creature, but to God alone, is to be made and performed with all religious care and faithfulness;[8] but popish monastical vows of perpetual single life,[9] professed poverty,[10] and regular obedience, are so far

from being degrees of higher perfection, that they are superstitious and sinful snares, in which no Christian may entangle himself.[11]

---

[1] Exodus 20:7; Deuteronomy 10:20; Jeremiah 4:2 [2] 2 Chronicles 6:22-23
[3] Matthew 5:34,37; James 5:12 [4] Hebrews 6:16; 2 Corinthians 1:23
[5] Nehemiah 13:25 [6] Leviticus 19:12; Jeremiah 23:10 [7] Psalm 24:4 [8] Psalm 76:11; Genesis 28:20-22 [9] 1 Corinthians 7:2,9 [10] Ephesians 4:28 [11] Matthew 19:1

CHAPTER 24:
THE CIVIL MAGISTRATE

1. God, the supreme Lord and King of all the world, has ordained civil magistrates to be under him, over the people, for his own glory and the public good; and to this end has armed them with the power of the sword, for defense and encouragement of them that do good, and for the punishment of evil doers.[1]

2. It is lawful for Christians to accept and execute the office of a magistrate when called thereunto; in the management whereof, as they ought especially to maintain justice and peace,[2] according to the wholesome laws of each kingdom and commonwealth, so for that end they may lawfully now, under the New Testament, wage war upon just and necessary occasions.[3]

3. Civil magistrates being set up by God for the ends aforesaid; subjection, in all lawful things commanded by them, ought to be yielded by us in the Lord, not only for wrath, but for conscience' sake;[4] and we ought to make supplications and prayers for kings and all that are in authority, that under them we may live a quiet and peaceable life, in all godliness and honesty.[5]

---

[1] Romans 13:1-4 [2] 2 Samuel 23:3; Psalm 82:3-4 [3] Luke 3:14 [4] Romans 13:5-7; 1 Peter 2:17 [5] 1 Timothy 2:1-2

CHAPTER 25:
MARRIAGE

1. Marriage is to be between one man and one woman; neither is it lawful for any man to have more than one wife, nor for any woman to have more than one husband at the same time.[1]

2. Marriage was ordained for the mutual help of husband and wife,[2] for the increase of mankind with a legitimate issue,[3] and the preventing of uncleanness.[4]

3. It is lawful for all sorts of people to marry, who are able with judgment to give their consent;[5] yet it is the duty of Christians to marry in the Lord;[6] and therefore such as profess the true religion, should not marry with infidels, or idolaters; neither should such as are godly, be unequally yoked, by marrying with such as are wicked in their life, or maintain damnable heresy.[7]

4. Marriage ought not to be within the degrees of consanguinity or affinity, forbidden in the Word;[8] nor can such incestuous marriages ever be made lawful, by any law of man or consent of parties, so as those persons may live together as man and wife.[9]

---

[1] Genesis 2:24; Malachi 2:15; Matthew 19:5-6 [2] Genesis 2:18 [3] Genesis 1:28
[4] 1 Corinthians 7:2,9 [5] Hebrews 13:4; 1 Timothy 4:3 [6] 1 Corinthians 7:39
[7] Nehemiah 13:25-27 [8] Leviticus 18 [9] Mark 6:18; 1 Corinthians 5:1

CHAPTER 26:
THE CHURCH

1. The catholic or universal church, which (with respect to the internal work of the Spirit and truth of grace) may be called invisible, consists of the whole number of the elect, that have been, are, or shall be gathered into one, under Christ, the head thereof; and is the spouse, the body, the fulness of him that fills all in all.[1]

2. All persons throughout the world, professing the faith of the gospel, and obedience unto God by Christ according unto it, not destroying their own profession by any errors everting the foundation, or unholiness of conversation, are and may be called visible saints;[2] and of such ought all particular congregations to be constituted.[3]

3. The purest churches under heaven are subject to mixture and error;[4] and some have so degenerated as to become no churches of Christ, but synagogues of Satan;[5] nevertheless Christ always has had, and ever shall have a kingdom in this world, to the end thereof, of such as believe in him, and make profession of his name.[6]

4. The Lord Jesus Christ is the Head of the church, in whom, by the appointment of the Father, all power for the calling, institution, order or government of the church, is invested in a supreme and sovereign manner;[7] neither can the Pope of Rome in any sense be head thereof, but is that antichrist, that man of sin, and son of perdition, that exalts himself in the

church against Christ, and all that is called God; whom the Lord shall destroy with the brightness of his coming.[8] (see note at the end of chapter 26)

5. In the execution of this power wherewith he is so intrusted, the Lord Jesus calls out of the world unto himself, through the ministry of his word, by his Spirit, those that are given unto him by his Father,[9] that they may walk before him in all the ways of obedience, which he prescribes to them in his word.[10] Those thus called, he commands to walk together in particular societies, or churches, for their mutual edification, and the due performance of that public worship, which he requires of them in the world.[11]

6. The members of these churches are saints by calling, visibly manifesting and evidencing (in and by their profession and walking) their obedience unto that call of Christ;[12] and do willingly consent to walk together, according to the appointment of Christ; giving up themselves to the Lord, and one to another, by the will of God, in professed subjection to the ordinances of the Gospel.[13]

7. To each of these churches therefore gathered, according to his mind declared in his word, he has given all that power and authority, which is in any way needful for their carrying on that order in worship and discipline, which he has instituted for them to observe; with commands and rules for the due and right exerting, and executing of that power.[14]

8. A particular church, gathered and completely organized according to the mind of Christ, consists of officers and members; and the officers appointed by Christ to be chosen and set apart by the church (so called and gathered), for the peculiar

administration of ordinances, and execution of power or duty, which he intrusts them with, or calls them to, to be continued to the end of the world, are bishops or elders, and deacons.[15]

9. The way appointed by Christ for the calling of any person, fitted and gifted by the Holy Spirit, unto the office of bishop or elder in a church, is, that he be chosen thereunto by the common suffrage of the church itself;[16] and solemnly set apart by fasting and prayer, with imposition of hands of the eldership of the church, if there be any before constituted therein;[17] and of a deacon that he be chosen by the like suffrage, and set apart by prayer, and the like imposition of hands.[18] (see note at the end of chapter 26)

10. The work of pastors being constantly to attend the service of Christ, in his churches, in the ministry of the word and prayer, with watching for their souls, as they that must give an account to Him;[19] it is incumbent on the churches to whom they minister, not only to give them all due respect, but also to communicate to them of all their good things according to their ability,[20] so as they may have a comfortable supply, without being themselves entangled in secular affairs;[21] and may also be capable of exercising hospitality towards others;[22] and this is required by the law of nature, and by the express order of our Lord Jesus, who has ordained that they that preach the Gospel should live of the Gospel.[23]

11. Although it be incumbent on the bishops or pastors of the churches, to be instant in preaching the word, by way of office, yet the work of preaching the word is not so peculiarly confined to them but that others also gifted and fitted by the Holy Spirit for it, and approved and called by the church, may and ought to perform it.[24]

12. As all believers are bound to join themselves to particular churches, when and where they have opportunity so to do; so all that are admitted unto the privileges of a church, are also under the censures and government thereof, according to the rule of Christ.[25]

13. No church members, upon any offence taken by them, having performed their duty required of them towards the person they are offended at, ought to disturb any church-order, or absent themselves from the assemblies of the church, or administration of any ordinances, upon the account of such offence at any of their fellow members, but to wait upon Christ, in the further proceeding of the church.[26]

14. As each church, and all the members of it, are bound to pray continually for the good and prosperity of all the churches of Christ,[27] in all places, and upon all occasions to further every one within the bounds of their places and callings, in the exercise of their gifts and graces, so the churches, when planted by the providence of God, so as they may enjoy opportunity and advantage for it, ought to hold communion among themselves, for their peace, increase of love, and mutual edification.[28]

15. In cases of difficulties or differences, either in point of doctrine or administration, wherein either the churches in general are concerned, or any one church, in their peace, union, and edification; or any member or members of any church are injured, in or by any proceedings in censures not agreeable to truth and order: it is according to the mind of Christ, that many churches holding communion together, do, by their messengers, meet to consider, and give their advice in or about that matter in difference, to be reported to all the churches concerned;[29] howbeit these messengers assembled,

are not intrusted with any church-power properly so called; or with any jurisdiction over the churches themselves, to exercise any censures either over any churches or persons; or to impose their determination on the churches or officers.[30]

---

1 Hebrews 12:23; Colossians 1:18; Ephesians 1:10,22-23, 5:23,27,32
2 1 Corinthians 1:2; Acts 11:26 **3** Romans 1:7; Ephesians 1:20-22 **4** 1 Corinthians 5; Revelation 2, 3 **5** Revelation 18:2; 2 Thessalonians 2:11-12 **6** Matthew 16:18; Psalm 72:17, 102:28; Revelation 12:17 **7** Colossians 1:18; Matthew 28:18-20; Ephesians 4:11-12 **8** 2 Thessalonians 2:2-9 **9** John 10:16; John 12:32
10 Matthew 28:20 **11** Matthew 18:15-20 **12** Romans 1:7; 1 Corinthians 1:2
13 Acts 2:41-42, 5:13-14; 2 Corinthians 9:13 **14** Matthew 18:17-18; 1 Corinthians 5:4-5,13; 2 Corinthians 2:6-8 **15** Acts 20:17,28; Philippians 1:1
16 Acts 14:23 **17** 1 Timothy 4:14 **18** Acts 6:3,5-6 **19** Acts 6:4; Hebrews 13:17
20 1 Timothy 5:17-18; Galatians 6:6-7 **21** 2 Timothy 2:4 **22** 1 Timothy 3:2
23 1 Corinthians 9:6-14 **24** Acts 11:19-21; 1 Peter 4:10-11
25 1 Thessalonians 5:14; 2 Thessalonians 3:6,14-15 **26** Matthew 18:15-17; Ephesians 4:2-3 **27** Ephesians 6:18; Psalm 122:6 **28** Romans 16:1-2; 3 John 8-10
29 Acts 15:2,4,6,22-23,25 **30** 2 Corinthians 1:24; 1 John 4:1

(Chapter 26, paragraph 4 equates the Pope of Rome with the antichrist. While we would agree that the Pope could be an antichrist by teaching a false gospel, to describe him in terms reserved for the antichrist is concluding too much.)

(Chapter 26, paragraph 9 reflects a congregational perspective on church government whereas some who utilize this confession are elder governed as per passages such as 1 Timothy 5:17 where they are described as those who "rule" or govern.)

CHAPTER 27:
THE COMMUNION OF SAINTS

1. All saints that are united to Jesus Christ, their head, by his Spirit, and faith, although they are not made thereby one person with him, have fellowship in his graces, sufferings, death, resurrection, and glory;[1] and, being united to one another in love, they have communion in each others gifts and graces,[2] and are obliged to the performance of such duties, public and private, in an orderly way, as do conduce to their mutual good, both in the inward and outward man.[3]

2. Saints by profession are bound to maintain a holy fellowship and communion in the worship of God, and in performing such other spiritual services as tend to their mutual edification;[4] as also in relieving each other in outward things according to their several abilities, and necessities;[5] which communion, according to the rule of the gospel, though especially to be exercised by them, in the relation wherein they stand, whether in families,[6] or churches,[7] yet, as God offers opportunity, is to be extended to all the household of faith, even all those who in every place call upon the name of the Lord Jesus; nevertheless their communion one with another as saints, does not take away or infringe the title or propriety which each man has in his goods and possessions.[8]

1 1 John 1:3; John 1:16; Philippians 3:10; Romans 6:5-6 **2** Ephesians 4:15-16; 1 Corinthians 12:7; 3:21-23 **3** 1 Thessalonians 5:11,14; Romans 1:12; 1 John 3:17-18; Galatians 6:10 **4** Hebrews 10:24-25, 3:12-13 **5** Acts 11:29-30 **6** Ephesians 6:4 **7** 1 Corinthians 12:14-27 **8** Acts 5:4; Ephesians 4:28

CHAPTER 28:
BAPTISM & THE LORD'S SUPPER

1. Baptism and the Lord's Supper are ordinances of positive and sovereign institution, appointed by the Lord Jesus, the only lawgiver, to be continued in his church to the end of the world.[1]

2. These holy appointments are to be administered by those only who are qualified and thereunto called, according to the commission of Christ.[2]

---

[1] Matthew 28:19-20; 1 Corinthians 11:26 [2] Matthew 28:19; 1 Corinthians 4:1

CHAPTER 29:
BAPTISM

1. Baptism is an ordinance of the New Testament, ordained by Jesus Christ, to be unto the party baptized, a sign of his fellowship with him, in his death and resurrection; of his being engrafted into him;[1] of remission of sins;[2] and of giving up into God, through Jesus Christ, to live and walk in newness of life.[3]

2. Those who do actually profess repentance towards God, faith in, and obedience to, our Lord Jesus Christ, are the only proper subjects of this ordinance.[4]

3. The outward element to be used in this ordinance is water, wherein the party is to be baptized, in the name of the Father, and of the Son, and of the Holy Spirit.[5]

4. Immersion, or dipping of the person in water, is necessary to the due administration of this ordinance.[6]

---

1 Romans 6:3-5; Colossians 2:12; Galatians 3:27 **2** Mark 1:4; Acts 22:16 **3** Romans 6:4 **4** Mark 16:16; Acts 8:36-37, 2:41, 8:12, 18:8 **5** Matthew 28:19-20; Acts 8:38 **6** Matthew 3:16; John 3:23

CHAPTER 30:
THE LORD'S SUPPER

1. The supper of the Lord Jesus was instituted by him the same night wherein he was betrayed, to be observed in his churches, unto the end of the world, for the perpetual remembrance, and showing to all the world the sacrifice of himself in his death,[1] confirmation of the faith of believers in all the benefits thereof, their spiritual nourishment, and growth in him, their further engagement in, and to all duties which they owe to him; and to be a bond and pledge of their communion with him, and with each other.[2]

2. In this ordinance Christ is not offered up to his Father, nor any real sacrifice made at all for remission of sin of the quick or dead, but only a memorial of that one offering up of himself by himself upon the cross, once for all;[3] and a spiritual oblation of all possible praise unto God for the same.[4] So that the popish sacrifice of the mass, as they call it, is most abominable, injurious to Christ's own sacrifice the alone propitiation for all the sins of the elect.

3. The Lord Jesus hath, in this ordinance, appointed his ministers to pray, and bless the elements of bread and wine, and thereby to set them apart from a common to a holy use, and to take and break the bread; to take the cup, and, they communicating also themselves, to give both to the communicants.[5]

4. The denial of the cup to the people, worshipping the elements, the lifting them up, or carrying them about for adoration,

and reserving them for any pretended religious use, are all contrary to the nature of this ordinance, and to the institution of Christ.[6]

5. The outward elements in this ordinance, duly set apart to the use ordained by Christ, have such relation to him crucified, as that truly, although in terms used figuratively, they are sometimes called by the names of the things they represent, in other words, the body and blood of Christ,[7] albeit, in substance and nature, they still remain truly and only bread and wine, as they were before.[8]

6. That doctrine which maintains a change of the substance of bread and wine, into the substance of Christ's body and blood, commonly called transubstantiation, by consecration of a priest, or by any other way, is repugnant not to Scripture alone,[9] but even to common sense and reason, overthrows the nature of the ordinance, and has been, and is, the cause of manifold superstitions, yea, of gross idolatries.[10]

7. Worthy receivers, outwardly partaking of the visible elements in this ordinance, do then also inwardly by faith, really and indeed, yet not carnally and corporally, but spiritually receive, and feed upon Christ crucified, and all the benefits of his death; the body and blood of Christ being then not corporally or carnally, but spiritually present to the faith of believers in that ordinance, as the elements themselves are to their outward senses.[11]

8. All ignorant and ungodly persons, as they are unfit to enjoy communion with Christ, so are they unworthy of the Lord's table, and cannot, without great sin against him, while they remain such, partake of these holy mysteries, or be admitted

thereunto;[12] yea, whosoever shall receive unworthily, are guilty of the body and blood of the Lord, eating and drinking judgment to themselves.[13]

---

1 1 Corinthians 11:23-26 **2** 1 Corinthians 10:16-17,21 **3** Hebrews 9:25-26,28
4 1 Corinthians 11:24; Matt. 26:26-27 **5** 1 Corinthians 11:23-26, etc.
6 Matthew 26:26-28, 15:9; Exodus 20:4-5 **7** 1 Corinthians 11:27
8 1 Corinthians 11:26-28 **9** Acts 3:21; Luke 14:6,39 **10** 1 Corinthians 11:24-25
11 1 Corinthians 10:16, 11:23-26 **12** 2 Corinthians 6:14-15
13 1 Corinthians 11:29; Matthew 7:6

CHAPTER 31:
MAN'S STATE AFTER DEATH, & THE RESURRECTION

1. The bodies of men after death return to dust, and see corruption;[1] but their souls, which neither die nor sleep, having an immortal subsistence, immediately return to God who gave them.[2] The souls of the righteous being then made perfect in holiness, are received into paradise, where they are with Christ, and behold the face of God in light and glory, waiting for the full redemption of their bodies;[3] and the souls of the wicked are cast into hell; where they remain in torment and utter darkness, reserved to the judgment of the great day;[4] besides these two places, for souls separated from their bodies, the Scripture acknowledgeth none.

2. At the last day, such of the saints as are found alive, shall not sleep, but be changed;[5] and all the dead shall be raised up with the selfsame bodies, and none other;[6] although with different qualities, which shall be united again to their souls forever.[7]

3. The bodies of the unjust shall, by the power of Christ, be raised to dishonour; the bodies of the just, by his Spirit, unto honour, and be made conformable to his own glorious body.[8]

---

[1] Genesis 3:19; Acts 13:36 [2] Ecclesiastes 12:7 [3] Luke 23:43; 2 Corinthians 5:1,6,8; Philippians 1:23; Hebrews 12:23 [4] Jude 6, 7; 1 Peter 3:19; Luke 16:23-24

5 1 Corinthians 15:51-52; 1 Thessalonians 4:17 **6** Job 19:26-27
7 1 Corinthians 15:42-43 **8** Acts 24:15; John 5:28-29; Philippians 3:21

CHAPTER 32:
THE FINAL JUDGEMENT

1. God has appointed a day wherein he will judge the world in righteousness, by Jesus Christ;[1] to whom all power and judgment is given of the Father; in which day, not only the apostate angels shall be judged,[2] but likewise all persons that have lived upon the earth shall appear before the tribunal of Christ, to give an account of their thoughts, words, and deeds, and to receive according to what they have done in the body, whether good or evil.[3]

2. The end of God's appointing this day, is for the manifestation of the glory of his mercy, in the eternal salvation of the elect; and of his justice, in the eternal damnation of the reprobate, who are wicked and disobedient;[4] for then shall the righteous go into everlasting life, and receive that fulness of joy and glory with everlasting rewards, in the presence of the Lord; but the wicked, who do not know God, and do not obey the gospel of Jesus Christ, shall be cast aside into everlasting torments,[5] and punished with everlasting destruction, from the presence of the Lord, and from the glory of his power.[6]

3. As Christ would have us to be certainly persuaded that there shall be a day of judgment, both to deter all men from sin,[7] and for the greater consolation of the godly in their adversity,[8] so will he have the day unknown to men, that they may shake off all carnal security, and be always watchful, because they know not at what hour the Lord will come,[9] and may ever be prepared to say, Come Lord Jesus; come quickly[10] Amen.

1 Acts 17:31; John 5:22,27 **2** 1 Corinthians 6:3; Jude 6 **3** 2 Corinthians 5:10; Ecclesiastes 12:14; Matthew 12:36; Romans 14:10,12; Matthew 25:32-46 **4** Romans 9:22-23 **5** Matthew 25:21,34; 2 Timothy 4:8 **6** Matthew 25:46; Mark 9:48; 2 Thessalonians 1:7-10 **7** 2 Corinthians 5:10-11 **8** 2 Thessalonians 1:5-7 **9** Mark 13:35-37; Luke 12:35-40 **10** Revelation 22:20

SUGGESTED RESOURCES

The Creedal Imperative by Carl Trueman
(Wheaton, IL: Good News Publishers), 2012.

The Utility and Importance of Creeds and Confessions
by Samuel Miller (Princeton, NJ: D. A. Borrenstein), 1824.

A Defense of Confessionalism by Arden L. Hodgins, Jr.
(Palmdale, CA: The Institute of Reformed Baptist Studies), 2016.

The Shape of Sola Scriptura by Keith A. Mathison
(Moscow, ID: Canon Press), 2001.